LOUISE A. MAUFFETTE-LEENDERS

JAMES A. ERSKINE

MICHIEL R. LEENDERS

learning
with
cases

fourth edition

D0753855

The Proven Guide

Learning with Cases
Fourth Edition

ISBN   978-0-7714-2584-4

This book may be ordered from:

Senton Incorporated
1669 Oxford Street East
London, Ontario, Canada,
N5V 2Z5

(+1) 800.455.9808
(+1) 519.455.5500
casemethodbooks@senton.com

casemethodbooks@gmail.com
www.casemethodbooks.com

The Case Centre
Cranfield University
Wharley End, Bedford
MK43 0JR, UK

+44 1234 750903

info@thecasecentre.org (UK)

info.usa@thecasecentre.org (US)
www.thecasecentre.org

about the authors

The author team has collectively taught case learning, writing and teaching workshops to over 20,000 participants in more than 50 countries.

Louise A. Mauffette-Leenders holds a BA from Collège Jean-de-Brébeuf, a BBA and MBA from l'École des Hautes Études Commerciales of Montréal, Québec. As case writer and research associate at The Richard Ivey School of Business at The University of Western Ontario, she wrote dozens of cases in all areas of management, including the non-profit sector. Since 1987, Louise has worked in social services and international development. She has written and taught cases in various training programs for social service providers.

James A. Erskine teaches Operations Management at the Richard Ivey School of Business where he has a special interest in the human in the system. He has Engineering and MBA degrees from The University of Western Ontario and a doctorate from Indiana University. Jim has served as Dean at the Lahore University of Management Sciences in Pakistan and is a past chairperson of the Honors Undergraduate Business Program at Ivey. He has been cited for distinguished contribution by both the World Association for Case Method Research and Application (WACRA) and the North American Case Research Association (NACRA). Jim is a 3-M Teaching Fellow recognizing him as one of Canada's best university professors.

Michiel R. Leenders is Professor Emertitus and holds the Leenders Purchasing Management Association of Canada Chair at the Richard Ivey School of Business. He received a degree in Mining Engineering from the University of Alberta, an MBA from The University of Western Ontario and his doctorate from the Harvard Business School. He is a former director of the School's Ph.D. program and teaches and consults internationally. He has authored and co-authored ten books in the supply management field translated into nine languages. In 1997, Mike received the Leaders in Management Education Award sponsored by the Financial Post and Bell Canada.

acknowledgements

The Harvard Business School's creation of the case method for use in management education has been one of its many successes. We wish to acknowledge especially the contribution of Professors Roland Christensen and Andrew Towl.

Participative teaching is impossible without motivated students in the classroom. It has been our good fortune to have had a constant stream of such talent. We wish to express our gratefulness to them collectively for their contributions to the development of the key ideas in this book.

All of our case method texts have been produced by Senton Printing and we appreciate their continuing efforts in all of the logistics associated with our books.

foreword

The Socratic method, on which the case method is based, has been around since antiquity. Nevertheless, I feel compelled to report that, even before the Harvard Business School adopted it for management education purposes, my great-grandfather, Joseph Octave Mauffette who, in 1880, founded Collège St-Joseph on Île Perrot, the first lay college of Quebec, was a fervent proponent of participative learning.

My treasured 1888 edition of the college calendar states (in French), "What most distinguishes this college from other institutions of the same type, what recommends it among all, and the key point to which we wish to draw attention is our use of the combined training system and Socratic method." My ancestor proceeds to explain that the use of books, lectures and essays is reduced to a minimum under this system. Knowledge originates from the pupils through the skillful questioning of the teacher and each truth thus derived becomes indelibly engraved in the pupils' minds. He concludes, "Our education goal is not to stuff our pupils' heads with facts of doubtful utility that they will likely forget as soon as they come out of college, but rather to instill practical knowledge and, above all, to allow them to grow into the habit of logical and correct reasoning in every subject."

I am proud to continue in the same lineage more than one hundred years later by offering you, along with my husband Mike and our colleague Jim, the fourth edition of this book that subscribes to a proven educational philosophy.

Louise A. Mauffette-Leenders

preface

This book is about learning by the case method. Written from a student perspective, it focuses on learning fast and effectively. It provides in-depth coverage of the three stage learning process: (1) individual preparation; (2) small group discussion; and (3) large group discussion. It also gives useful aids through the Case Difficulty Cube, the Short and Long Cycle Processes of individual preparation, the Case Preparation Chart; and suggestions for small and large group effectiveness as well as case presentations, reports and exams. This text focuses on a professional and ethical approach to learning, invaluable for those who wish to distinguish themselves in their future careers.

The case method has evolved considerably since the Harvard Business School introduced it in the first decades of the twentieth century. Subsequently, a vast number of business programs have adopted this method, to some degree, not only in North America but also in the rest of the world. The growth in the number of requests we have received to give case writing and case teaching workshops around the globe confirms continuing interest. Moreover, the case method is used in an ever increasing number of disciplines aside from management education. Whenever people have to learn how to make complex decisions, the case method is effective.

While some documentation on the case method exists, most of it is written from a teaching perspective. Resources to assist students in using this method are scarce and fragmentary. Typically, they consist of a short handout or a few comments delivered in the beginning of a course or program. Until this text no comprehensive guide existed covering all key aspects of learning with cases. Our goal is to help students get the most out of their case learning experience without spending excessive time.

Learning with Cases completes our trilogy. Our other two texts on the case method, *Writing Cases* and *Teaching with Cases,* present the state of the art with respect to case writing and teaching. *Learning with Cases* is based on a review of existing literature and on our own ideas originating from over one hundred years of combined experience not only in teaching thousands of students and executives by the case method, but also in writing hundreds of cases, and in training countless educators locally and throughout the world.

Since the third edition of *Learning with Cases*, we published translations in French, *Apprendre cas par cas*, and in Spanish, *Aprende con casos*.

contents

CHAPTER 1: CASES AND THE CASE METHOD 1
What Is a Case? 2
Why Are Cases Used? 3
    Inventory of Skills Developed by the Case Method 5
What Is Expected of You in the Case Method? 7
    1. Take an active role in your learning. 7
    2. Follow a code of professional conduct 7
    3. Commit yourself to ongoing learning. 7
How to Use This Book Effectively 8
A Note about Language 8
A Look Ahead. 9

CHAPTER 2: THE CASE DIFFICULTY CUBE AND THE
                THREE STAGE LEARNING PROCESS 11
The Educational Challenge of a Case and
the Case Difficulty Cube 11
    The Analytical Dimension 12
    The Conceptual Dimension. 14
    The Presentation Dimension 15
    The Case Difficulty Cube 16
The Three Stage Process of Learning with Cases. 18
    Stage 1- Individual Preparation 20
    Stage 2- Small Group Discussion 21
    Stage 3- Large Group Discussion 24
After Class Reflection 27
Conclusion 28

CHAPTER 3: INDIVIDUAL PREPARATION 29
Case Assignments 30
    The Standard Assignment Question 30
    Other Types of Assignments 31
    Beyond the Assignment Questions 32
The Short Cycle Process 32
The Long Cycle Process 35
    Part 1: Detailed Reading of the Case 37
    Part 2: Analyze the Case. 40
        A) Define the Issue. 41

B) Analyze Case Data 43
C) Generate Alternatives 46
D) Select Decision Criteria 47
E) Assess Alternatives 49
F) Select Preferred Alternative. 52
G) Develop an Action and Implementation Plan 53
Missing Information and Assumptions 54
Evaluating Results. 56
Tips for Effective Individual Preparation 57
The Case Preparation Chart 59

CHAPTER 4: SMALL GROUP DISCUSSION 61
Organizing for Effective Small Group Work. 62
Size 62
Composition. 63
Rotation 63
Time 64
Timing 65
Location 65
Establishing Small Group Guidelines 65
Discussing in the Small Group 67
Identifying Small Group Problems. 68
Dealing with Small Group Problems. 70
Reflecting on the Small Group and Preparing Your Class
Contribution Agenda 72

CHAPTER 5: LARGE GROUP DISCUSSION 75
The Large Group or Class Discussion Process 76
1. In-Class - Pre-Class 76
2. Pre-Case or "Warm-up" 77
3. The Case Discussion. 78
4. Post-Case or Closing. 82
Stakeholders in the Classroom Discussion Process 84
The Instructor. 84
The Participants. 85
Participation in the Large Group Discussion 85
Effective Participation. 86
Ineffective Participation 89
Personal Strategies and Tactics for
Managing Your Contributions 91

Inputs to Class 92
Effective Listening 93
Note-Taking 94
Dealing with Specific Challenges to Participation 95
After Class Reflection 99
Ethical Considerations. 100

**CHAPTER 6: CASE PRESENTATIONS, REPORTS AND
EXAMS**. 103
Case Presentations 103
Types of Presentation 103
Suggestions for Effective Presentations. 105
Suggestions for Critic-Observers 106
Case reports 107
Types of Report 107
Suggestions for Effective Case Reports 108
Case Exams 111
Types of Exam 111
Suggestions on How to Prepare and
Write an In-Class Exam 112
A) With the Case Handed out Ahead of Time 112
B) With the Case Handed out at the Start of the Exam 113
Suggestions that Apply to All Types of Case Exams . . . 114
A Note about Grades for Written Work 117

**CHAPTER 7: MANAGING YOUR LEARNING
PROCESS**. 119
Cases and the Case Method 120
The Two Key Frameworks 120
The Case Difficulty Cube. 120
The Three Stage Learning Process 121
Individual Preparation 123
Small Group Discussion 125
Large Group Discussion 126
Variations 127
Conclusion 128

REFERENCES. 130

INDEX 132

cases and the case method

For the first time in my life, learning is relevant and actually fun.

By putting myself in the shoes of various decision makers, I am rehearsing for my future career.

This is not fiction. I know these cases are real. I get a chance to learn firsthand and to practice all kinds of skills I'll need in my job.

The excitement and satisfaction one can sense from these actual comments are typical of participants in the case learning process enrolled in under-graduate, graduate and executive programs alike. You can feel the same way about learning with cases, provided you follow the ideas presented in this book.

The goal of this book is to help you maximize your learning with cases within a reasonable amount of time. Faithfully repeating a three stage learning process of individual preparation, small group discussion and large group discussion will enable you to become a more successful professional in your chosen career.

A useful way for you to start is to develop an understanding of what a case really is, why cases are valuable learning tools, and what is expected of you.

WHAT IS A CASE?

A case is a description of an actual situation, commonly involving a decision, a challenge, an opportunity, a problem or an issue faced by a person (or persons) in an organization. A case allows you to step figuratively into the position of a particular decision maker.

Cases are normally written and appear in print form. Increasingly, they are also presented in other formats such as film, video tape, CD ROM, audio tape, disk, or a combination of these. With interactive computer graphics, communications networks and hypermedia databases, cases can engage participants in novel ways. However, hard copy cases remain the most common type because of cost and convenience.

Cases are field-based. A case researcher visits an organization and collects the data that comprise the case. Moreover, someone in this organization signs an official release document. It is this release that truly distinguishes cases from any other kind of educational material. The release serves four purposes: First, it guarantees that the case writer has in fact gone to the field and done the work required to write someone else's story, as opposed to writing stories from the security of one's office in a comfortable "arm-chair." Second, it authenticates the story. A signed release says that the situation is accurately and fairly portrayed. It is not unusual for cases to be disguised at the request of the person granting release. Some case information, such as names of the organization and people, may be changed to assure confidentiality but every effort has been taken to make certain the key issue and its context have been properly preserved. Third, the release grants permission to use the case for educational purposes. And fourth, the release helps maintain positive relations between the educational institution and the people and organizations about which cases are written.

Other educational materials such as an exercise, a problem, an article or a simulation are different from a case in that the writer or author may not have used real life data and obtained a release. Sometimes these materials are improperly referred to as cases and occasionally bear the label of "armchair cases."

Cases are the product of a carefully thought-out process. Although a case contains the information available to the decision maker at the time it is developed, the content varies with the educational purpose of the case. Following specific teaching objectives, the case researcher reports the information about the decision faced by the focal person of the case. Obviously, not everything that is seen or heard can be included and the researcher has to be selective.

As a matter of fact, a large part of the case remains unwritten. For example, the economic, social, political and technological context of the case is implied by its date and location. And this unwritten context is almost always relevant to the analysis and solution of the case. You are expected to bring your own context understanding and experience to bear on the case.

WHY ARE CASES USED?

Cases enable you to learn by doing and by teaching others. What you learn becomes deeply ingrained and stays with you. The repetitive opportunity to identify, analyze and solve a number of issues in a variety of settings prepares you to become truly professional in your field of work.

The whole point behind using cases is to allow you to take on the roles and responsibilities of specific people in specific organizations. Think of it as a form of on-the-job training. Cases provide an opportunity to become deeply involved in decisions actually faced by real people in real organizations; to take ownership, to feel the pressure, to recognize the risks, and to expose your ideas to others. Please recognize that the real life people, whose roles you assume in cases, were under pressure, may have felt butterflies in their stomachs and, in some instances, put their careers on the line.

Just imagine the experience you will accumulate over time while addressing these issues and challenges across a wide range of functional areas, levels of responsibilities, types and sizes of organizations and industries, as well as locations throughout the world.

There is a wealth of learning opportunities in each case that you unlock each time you put yourself into the decision maker's position. It is the cumulative impact of these different case challenges that will permit you to take on future tasks knowing that the process of tackling decisions effectively has become a major personal asset.

Cases give you a chance to practice the art as well as the science of management in a laboratory setting, with little corporate and personal risk involved. In essence, cases are to management students what cadavers are to medical students, the opportunity to practice on the real thing harmlessly.

Cases are also an excellent tool to test the understanding of theory, to connect theory with application, and to develop theoretical insights. Cases themselves may contain theoretical materials or readings may be assigned in conjunction with cases to cover theoretical perspectives. Cases provide the opportunity to see how theory applies in practice.

Moreover, cases provide information about how work is planned and organized in various settings, how systems operate and how organizations compete.

Managers seldom have access to all the information pertinent to decisions. Likewise, cases seldom contain all the information you would like. Thus cases force you to make decisions with available information, thereby helping you to tolerate incompleteness of information and ambiguity.

Because of the discussion-based format of the case method, cases are an excellent vehicle for developing your self-confidence and your ability to think independently and work cooperatively. Moreover, cases foster the development of insights into your own strengths and weaknesses and allow for profound personal growth.

The case method of instruction is particularly well suited to deal with new and complex situations. In the business world in particular, managers need to adapt to ever changing circumstances. Cases force you to think for yourself and generate your own learning. Cases actually engage you in a process of learning how to learn. While every case is different, it is the process of learning how to learn that is generalizable.

Learning with cases provides you the opportunity to develop a wide range of very useful skills.

Inventory of Skills Developed by the Case Method

1. *Analytical skills.* The case method enables you to develop qualitative and quantitative frameworks to analyze business situations, including problem identification skills; data handling skills; and critical thinking skills. You are forced to reason clearly and logically in sifting carefully through the data available.

2. *Decision making skills.* The case method pushes you, on the basis of your analytical work, to assess what can be done and to make decisions. You will learn to generate different alternatives, to select decision criteria, to evaluate alternatives, to choose the best one, and to formulate congruent action and implementation plans.

3. *Application skills.* Cases provide an opportunity for you to practice using the tools, techniques, and theories you have learned.

4. *Oral communication skills.* The case method provides ample opportunity not only to listen to your colleagues but also to express yourself, construct arguments and convince them of your views. Thus, a whole set of speaking, listening and debating skills are developed. In this exchange of ideas and arguments, you learn to think on your feet, consider others' viewpoints as well as to take and defend your positions.

5. *Time management skills.* Under the heavy pressure of case preparation and the juggling of your various other responsibilities, you are forced to schedule educational activities carefully and manage time effectively.

6. *Interpersonal or social skills.* The case method, through small group and large group discussion, promotes learning how to deal with your peers. This learning includes conflict resolution skills and the art of compromise. Because so much of your future work life will involve committees, task forces, boards or project teams, learning to work effectively in a group will differentiate you.

7. *Creative skills.* Because no two business situations are quite the same, the case method encourages looking for and finding solutions geared to the unique circumstances of each case. This method invites you also to use your imagination in problem solving, as there are normally multiple solutions to each case.

8. *Written communication skills.* Through regular and effective note-taking, case reports and case exams, you learn the skills associated with effective writing. Emphasis on writing skills varies depending on the program you are enrolled in but often takes on a high priority in business programs, as a key factor of success in management.

WHAT IS EXPECTED OF YOU IN THE CASE METHOD?

In order to gain the various benefits of the case method and to develop all the skills listed above, you are encouraged to fulfill three expectations.

1. Take an active role in your learning.

If you are serious about learning with cases, you have no choice but to take an active role in your learning. The output depends strictly on your input.

You must come prepared for each class. You also must contribute to the learning of the group:

a) by teaching others;
b) by actively participating;
c) by taking risks;
d) by learning from your instructor and classmates.

2. Follow a code of professional conduct.

A second set of expectations relates to ethics. For learning to flourish, it is essential that it be anchored in a climate of genuine respect, trust, and openness. As future managers and business leaders, you are called upon to behave in a professional manner. This sense of professionalism not only involves conducting yourself with civility towards your peers and with openness towards diversity, but also respecting the confidentiality of case discussions and notes.

3. Commit yourself to ongoing learning.

The third expectation relates to the underlying theme throughout this book. To maximize effective learning with cases, you must be committed to continuous improvement, individually, in small groups as well as in the classroom. It is the faithful, regular repetition of the learning process, and the unremitting sharpening of your skills that will produce stellar achievement.

HOW TO USE THIS BOOK EFFECTIVELY

This book intends to be a comprehensive guide, a road map, with practical advice, suggestions and reminders to maximize your effective learning with cases.

We suggest that you read this book carefully all the way through to get a complete overview and understanding of the learning process it presents. Subsequently, we invite you to go back to it on a regular basis to review a specific topic or part of the process, and to make sure that you are on the right learning track.

For ease of access, we have made extensive use of headings, cross references and exhibits.

A NOTE ABOUT LANGUAGE

Some words related to the use of cases will crop up over and over again and may be used interchangeably.

The word *decision* will often be used to describe an issue, challenge, problem or opportunity faced by the key person in the case. The decision may also be a recommendation. Then the decision becomes what to recommend to others who may have the final decision or who collectively need to decide.

A *participant* will denote a student, case reader or any person engaged in the case learning process.

An *instructor*, teacher, facilitator, discussion leader, or professor is someone who has program, course, seminar or workshop instructional responsibilities.

A *case writer*, or author or researcher refers to the person who produced the case.

A *small group* may also be referred to as a study group, learning team, syndicate, or break-out group.

A *large group* discussion is often referred to as a class discussion or plenary session.

A LOOK AHEAD

The next chapter will present the Case Difficulty Cube and the three stage learning process. The three subsequent chapters will focus on each stage of this process: individual preparation in Chapter 3; small group discussion in Chapter 4; and large group discussion in Chapter 5. Chapter 6 will cover other uses for cases, such as presentations, reports and exams. Chapter 7, our last chapter, will review the highlights in learning with cases.

We invite you to adopt the models and try out the ideas presented in this book. And we hope that you will find *Learning with Cases* a most rewarding experience.

the case difficulty cube and the three stage learning process

Your learning is far more enjoyable if you are convinced that what you are learning and how you are learning it make sense. Therefore, two frameworks are developed here to help you learn with cases: (1) an insight into the educational challenge presented in a case and how that challenge is translated into a Case Difficulty Cube; (2) an overview of the three stage learning process that forms the core of this text.

Participants in a case learning experience are always constrained by time. It takes time to read, analyze, and discuss each case. Your goal is learning how to prepare cases quickly and well. To reach this goal you need to: (1) have a better understanding of where to spend time on each case; and (2) develop a process for tackling cases that helps you achieve consistently superior results.

THE EDUCATIONAL CHALLENGE OF A CASE AND THE CASE DIFFICULTY CUBE

The difficulty or the educational challenge of a case can be viewed as having at least three major dimensions: analytical, conceptual and presentation. Each dimension has three degrees of difficulty. In Exhibit 2-1 the analytical dimension is the A axis, the conceptual dimension the C axis and the presentation dimension the P axis.

Exhibit 2-1
THE THREE DIMENSIONS OF CASE DIFFICULTY

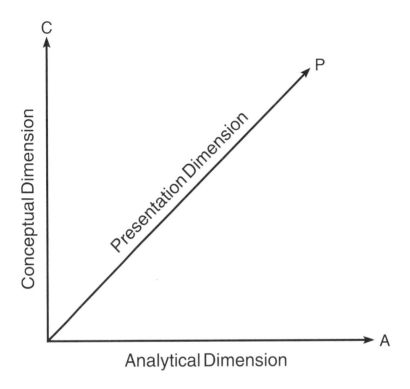

The Analytical Dimension

The analytical dimension of a case raises the question, "What is the case reader's task with respect to the key decision or issue of the case?" The analytical task depends on how the decision is presented in the case.

The case may be written with the issue stated, plus the alternatives considered, the decision criteria used and the final decision taken. For example, "Susan Lee, the finance manager of Excelsior Inc., was seeking additional funds for an expansion project and, after considering debt and equity options, decided that borrowing the money was the best decision." The participant's task becomes to assess whether the decision taken was, indeed, appropriate and the process followed correct, whether further alternatives might have been considered and what future consequences could be.

This kind of case has an analytical difficulty degree of one. In other words, the participant's task is about as easy as it can get on the analytical dimension. By the way, these cases tend to be dull. Most participants in the case learning process recognize that by the time they get a chance to study a case, the situation described in the case has probably been decided in real life. Nevertheless, there is a difference between realizing this and being told so in the case. It is a bit difficult to work assiduously on these one degree of difficulty cases when you have already been given the final decision actually taken.

A case may be written about exactly the same issue, either with or without some alternatives provided, but excluding the final decision taken. This type of case is the second degree of analytical difficulty, the one most commonly encountered in cases. Using the example of Ms. Lee, above, the case would be presented as follows: "Ms. Lee, the finance manager at Excelsior Inc., was seeking additional funds for an expansion project and wanted to determine whether debt or equity financing would be the best way to secure new capital." The participant's task is now to analyze the situation, generate additional alternatives, evaluate all alternatives against specified decision criteria, make a decision, and develop an action and implementation plan.

A case moves to the third degree of analytical difficulty when even the decision that needs to be made is not identified. There is only a description of a situation. For example, "Ms. Lee, finance manager of Excelsior Inc., was reviewing the corporation's current financial position." Now the participant's task becomes to analyze the situation, figure out whether a decision (or more) needs to be taken and what alternatives might be considered, what decision criteria should be applied and which alternative is preferable, how it might be implemented and what the outcomes are likely to be. This third degree of analytical difficulty requires a lot of work!

Thus, the way the decision is framed in the case can represent different degrees of analytical difficulty for the participant. Presumably, the more difficult the analytical dimension, the more analytical time the case will require.

The Conceptual Dimension

The conceptual or theoretical dimension of the case is concerned with the question, "What theories, concepts or techniques might be useful in the understanding and/or resolution of this case situation?"

Concepts or theoretical perspectives may be contained in chapters or article readings assigned with the case, or in the case itself. They may also have been covered earlier in the course or in other courses. Or they may come after the case, once the necessity for the theoretical perspective is established through the case. At the time of course design, the educator makes a decision as to how best to integrate the concepts or theory in a practical sense using a case. Cases often present and illustrate more concepts, theories, or techniques than most people realize.

Like the analytical dimension, the conceptual dimension of the case is divided into three degrees of difficulty. Difficulty in a conceptual sense has two aspects. First, how difficult is the concept or theory in or of itself? Can someone new to this idea understand it from just carefully reading about it in a textbook or an article without further class explanation? If so, this concept is simple and assigned the first degree of difficulty. Second, conceptual difficulty relates to the number of concepts to be used simultaneously to address the decision(s) or issue(s) on which the case is focused. One or two simple concepts constitute a difficulty degree of one.

One can easily see what increases the degree of conceptual difficulty in a case. The simple concept becomes complex, requiring extensive and repeated discussion and explanation in class, sometimes to the extent of lectures and/or problems or exercises. The single concept becomes many. This is why integrative courses, requiring a variety of other prerequisite courses and theoretical material, tend to have a significant level of conceptual difficulty.

Participants in the case study process require time to learn what the relevant conceptual or theoretical constructs are and how they might be applied in the context of each case. Conceptual difficulty is a relative notion. What may be difficult for some may not be equally difficult for others who are either adept at grasping a particular concept or who may have learned it earlier.

Taking some time to reflect on what concepts, theories or techniques are being raised in the case helps you prepare the foundation for your analysis.

The Presentation Dimension

The third educational challenge in a case relates to the presentation dimension which provides an opportunity to develop skills in sorting and structuring information. It raises the question, "What is really important and relevant information here and what is still missing?"

The presentation dimension is also divided into three degrees of difficulty. At the first degree of difficulty the case:

1. is short;
2. is well-organized;
3. contains almost all relevant information;
4. contains little extraneous information;
5. is conveyed in a single, simple format, most often written.

Such a case can be read quickly and relevant information is accessed easily. Indeed, one of the criticisms of the case method is exactly on this point. The argument is that in real life problems and decisions do not come to the decision maker in such a nice, clean, well-organized fashion. Actually, well organized cases are useful for educational purposes, since they allow concentration on the other two dimensions of case difficulty without burdening students with a massive presentation challenge.

One can easily see that the degree of difficulty related to the presentation of the case can be increased by changing up to all five of the previously mentioned points. Thus:

1. short becomes long;
2. well-organized becomes disorganized;
3. available relevant information becomes missing relevant information;
4. little extraneous information becomes a lot of extraneous information;
5. a single format, probably written, becomes multiple formats such as written, plus video, plus database or whatever.

The greater the degree of difficulty in the presentation dimension, the longer the participant needs to spend on reading, sorting, prioritizing, identifying missing information, and organizing and structuring data. All of these are necessary and useful skills.

The Case Difficulty Cube

Three degrees of difficulty along each of the three axes create a cube containing 27 sub-cubes (see Exhibit 2-2). Thus a (3, 3, 3) case is one where the learner will be challenged to identify the problem; may have difficulty understanding the concepts or theories which need to be used; and encounters additional difficulty because the case is long, with a lot of extraneous information and, possibly, not clearly presented. Such cases are often used near the end of courses or programs.

Exhibit 2-2
THE CASE DIFFICULTY CUBE

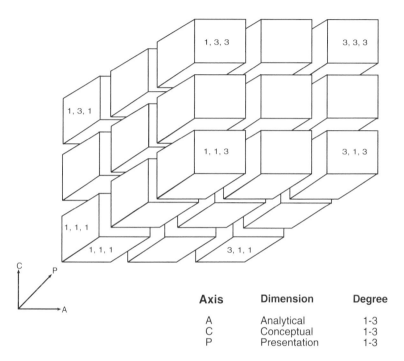

Axis	Dimension	Degree
A	Analytical	1-3
C	Conceptual	1-3
P	Presentation	1-3

In contrast a (1, 1, 1) case is relatively simple and straight-forward on each dimension. It identifies the problem and a solution, is simple in concept, and contains relevant, clearly presented material. Such cases are often used in the beginning of courses or programs.

A total measure of case difficulty may be established by using the arithmetic sum of the three dimensions. A total difficulty of 3 to 6, for example, ranges from easy at 3 to medium at 6. From 7 to 9 the case would be on the upper end of the difficulty scale. You may encounter (3, 3, 3) types of cases that may, at first, look impossibly difficult. Rather than giving up without trying, you will find that the approach suggested in this book will allow you to make a reasonable start, even if total comprehension may not be achievable in the time available.

Understanding the difficulty cube position of a case allows you to allocate preparation time appropriately. A (3, 1, 1) case obviously needs more time on the analytical dimension than the other two dimensions. A (1, 3, 1) case requires significant concentration on the conceptual dimension and may be thought of as a "short read, long think" type of case. A (1, 1, 3) case needs a major information sorting and specifying effort. A (3, 3, 3) case will require an extraordinary amount of time and effort on all three dimensions.

The Case Difficulty Cube is a useful aid to help you focus your learning efforts on the most challenging dimensions of a case. The second framework in this chapter relates your quantity and quality of learning to the three stage learning process.

THE THREE STAGE PROCESS OF
LEARNING WITH CASES

What a participant does with a case, once assigned, can be viewed as a process. The better that process is executed, the more rewarding the case learning experience becomes.

The case learning process is composed of three stages:

1. Individual Preparation
2. Small Group Discussion
3. Large Group or Class Discussion

Exhibit 2-3
THE THREE STAGE LEARNING PROCESS

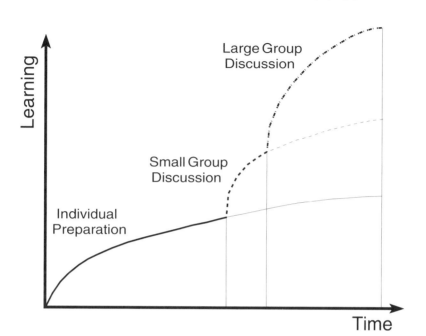

Each of these three stages is vital to effective learning and each contributes in different ways to maximizing the quantity and quality of learning. Exhibit 2-3 is a key diagram. It shows how each of the three stages contributes to the quality and quantity of your learning in a progressive and cumulative fashion. The aim is to help you achieve the best possible results in a minimum amount of time. The combination of all three stages, executed properly and in the correct sequence, assures effective learning. The following three chapters provide guidance and specific advice on how to execute these three stages. The introductory treatment in this chapter covers the basic logic as to why these stages are necessary and how they contribute to effective learning.

Stage 1 - Individual Preparation

In learning with cases, individual preparation is the first step. It is the basis for all subsequent work and hence, the foundation on which quality and quantity of case learning depend. In individual preparation you take on the role and responsibilities of the decision maker in the case and the task of solving the issue confronting you. Thus you have to become acquainted with the information contained in the case, normally by reading. Next follows an analytical and case solving process. Also, if theoretical concepts are relevant to the case, additional readings might be helpful in the analysis and resolution of the case. As you will discover, the reading of the case and theoretical material is not a standard perusal of information. It is focused and selective. It forces the reader into the position and role of the decision maker in the case.

Note that you are not asked to take on the personality and gender of the individual in the case. The intent is to imagine the decision maker as lifted out of the situation at the time of the case and the reader as having moved in. Thus, you bring personal skills and background along with biases to the situation at hand. The decision or issue or opportunity becomes yours and yours alone during the individual preparation stage. The acceptance of this role and responsibility transfer is one of the major challenges in the use of cases. It is so much more comfortable to stay as an observer or commentator about the case situation. It is so easy to slip from owner to outsider role. "I think that the key person in the case should do this" is much less threatening than "I would do this under these circumstances." The earlier during the reading phase this acceptance of ownership of the situation and role takes place the better.

Good individual preparation demands a high level of self-discipline and hard work. There has to be hunger and commitment behind this search for the right analysis, solution and implementation. It is related not only to true ownership of the case decision maker's role but also to individual motivation to do one's best. A simple way of thinking about it would be to compare it to the real life situation. "If I got fired if I made the wrong decision and promoted if I made the right one, how hard would I be working on this decision?" If real people in real life lost sleep about this situation and felt under pressure, is it not appropriate that this tension and stress also be felt by the ones that are supposed to be learning from this real life experience?

"How much can I accomplish alone within the time available?" is the continuing challenge in individual preparation. It is tempting to lean too heavily on the subsequent small and large group discussions to provide the answers. Nevertheless, there is great satisfaction in learning to "crack a case" on your own and becoming capable of doing the lion's share of the case analysis without the assistance of others.

Obviously, the better the individual preparation, the easier the following stages become.

Stage 2 - Small Group Discussion

Small group discussion provides a vital link between individual preparation and class or large group discussion. Yet, curiously, it is the one step most frequently left out because many educators and students do not recognize the contribution of this step to the whole learning process. Below are eight reasons why you should make it a standard practice to have a small group discussion of every case.

1.   Teach Others

There is no better way to learn than having to teach others. The small group discussion provides each participant with the first test of the individual preparation, "Do I really understand the issue and role I have taken over?" There is a huge difference between thinking you understand something and having to prove it. The whole process of learning with cases is based on the philosophy that you learn better by being actively involved in your own learning. If you can teach someone else what you know about a case so that the other person understands what you are talking about, then you also know.

2. Encourage Individual Preparation

It is the duty of every member to participate in the small group discussion. Peer pressure is strong on individuals in the group to prepare properly. Although it is possible for a student to hide lack of preparation in a large class, it is impossible to hide lack of preparation in a small group. Small group discussion is an opportunity to check insights, assumptions, and preparation against those of others; clarify understanding; listen attentively and critically to others; and argue for positions based on convictions developed during the individual preparation stage.

3. Speak about Every Case

Small group discussion provides the only chance for every member to speak about every case. There may not be enough time or opportunity in the large group discussion for every class member to get a chance to speak. Participating in the case learning process without getting an opportunity to talk about each case with others loses a lot of value. Knowing that one will not have a chance to talk about the case dulls the senses, turns individual preparation into a meaningless chore and the class discussion into a bore.

4. Develop Communication Skills

Small group discussion will give you practice in speaking, listening and other communication skills. Everyone gets to talk in the small group. Just as for musicians, actors or athletes, practicing is the only way to achieve high performance levels.

5. Recognize Good Ideas

It is just as important to learn to recognize good ideas as to be the originator of good ideas oneself. Being able to compare one's own ideas against those of others is a basic management skill fostered by cases.

6. Foster Effective Teamwork

Effective teamwork is fundamental to organizational success and participating in small groups provides valuable practice in learning to contribute to team success.

7. Build Confidence

Small groups also build confidence in each participant by showing that his or her understanding and analysis of the case is reasonable. Small group discussion makes it easier to debate viewpoints in the intimacy and safety of a small group than in front of the whole class. The classroom discussion process can be highly threatening to many; whereas the small group can provide a level of comfort when ideas generated in individual preparation and in the small group have merit and can, therefore, be safely voiced in a large group.

8. Build Relationships

Many past participants in the process of learning with cases remember fondly their small group discussions as a significant source of learning. Many also develop life long relationships with their group members.

As you can see, small group discussion is also tough. It requires constant alertness, a willingness to give and take, an ability to work both for the group and oneself and to share a common task quickly and effectively.

Please note that small group discussion is not a "now that we have all read the case, let's prepare it together" session. This bad habit requires too much time and absolves each individual of thorough individual preparation. The small group discussion is instead a shared effort to help one another to understand the case situation better, to use the group synergy to see how far the group can push beyond the analysis reached by its members individually. This discussion is a critical, as well as a caring process. "I am here to help you, but that may also mean I may not agree with you and I will tell you why." A good small group discussion will complement and add to the individual preparation. It will bring a burst of new ideas that would have taken a lot more time for an individual to uncover alone.

It does not matter if some of the points you make in the small group never get raised in the classroom. Remember, you are responsible for your own learning. Be assured that your serious and active involvement in the small group will pay high dividends in terms of developing your professional skills.

Small group time should be short and effective. The purpose is not to "kill" the case. The placing of the small group activity right between individual preparation and class recognizes that still more learning will follow. However, the art is to push the learning as far as possible within the time available so that the large group discussion can start at a higher plane.

Stage 3 - Large Group Discussion

Large group or class discussion is the final step in the three stage case learning process. Apart from later reviews, class discussion provides the last significant chance to develop a thorough understanding of the case. The learning diagram in Exhibit 2-3 makes it very clear that it is probably impossible for any individual or small group preparation to reach the level of understanding achievable at the end of the class. If, collectively, the class cannot push the total quality and quantity of learning beyond the level achieved in the individual and small group sessions, the class has not been a good one.

Inexperienced participants often feel frustrated by the seemingly inadequate levels of individual and small group accomplishment. Recognize that, in the first place, the key question at the end of the class discussion is, "Do I now understand what this whole situation is all about?" If the answer is "no," please make sure to find out from your instructor or a classmate why you still cannot comprehend the case after the large group discussion. If the answer is "yes," then the next questions become: (1) "In view of my understanding at the end of this class, what insights have I gained that can help me prepare better in the future?" and (2) "What can we do to have better small group discussions?"

This critical and ongoing feedback loop is essential to making the learning process continually improvable. Over time, the gap between the quality and quantity of learning achieved during individual preparation and small group discussion, and that achieved at the end of the class should be narrowing. If it is not, the feedback loop is not working very well.

The purpose of the class is not only just to reach a thorough understanding of the case and an optimal resolution of the issue or decision. The class discussion also gives class members the opportunity to practice in the large group, to share their individual and small group learning with others and to be evaluated by peers and instructors.

Fear of participating in the class discussion may stem from two major sources:

1. Inadequate individual preparation and small group work create fear. "You don't hide ignorance by talking" was one of the favorite sayings of Bud Wild, former head of the journalism department at our university. This kind of fear obviously can be handled by proper preparation.

    Clearly, this does not mean that only the "right" answers are acceptable in class. From a teaching-learning perspective "wrong" answers can frequently provide a valuable insight. In education, as in sports, practice means mistakes will occur and have to occur for true learning to take place.

2. An individual may find it difficult to speak up in a large group, regardless of the quality of prior preparation. Cultural, social and psychological factors may further reinforce personal reluctance to speak in class. This second kind of difficulty in speaking in the large group is tougher to deal with than the first. The first can be solved by adequate preparation. The second requires behavior modification. In Chapter 5 specific suggestions are given to help those who fall in this second category.

There are at least seven very good reasons why you should be prepared to participate in the large group.

1. *Learn by Doing*

Learning by doing is an essential part of the learning process. Knowing that one may have to participate in the large group discussion sharpens individual preparation, small group discussion and the quality of listening in the large group.

2. *Respond as Requested*

Instructors may ask you to participate.

3. *Teach Others*

Everyone in the class has the responsibility to help others to learn. Unwillingness to teach others and to share your insights prevents the class from having a superior learning experience. It also sends a message that you prefer to be a sponge; you will feed off the input of others but not contribute your share. Non-participation is often viewed as a lack of interest or a lack of care for the well-being and learning of your team, which will not do much for your reputation or acceptance among your classmates. Given that your classmates may become a significant part of your post-graduation network, their opinion of you may have long term consequences.

4. Practice Public Speaking

Many managers are called upon as part of their duties to present their views in front of others, whether they be employees, peers, superiors, a public, or the media. Public speaking skills are essential for any management position.

5. Be Included

It is more fun to be part of the group and included in the process.

6. Test Ideas

You may never know if your ideas were good enough to stand the rigor of class exposure. Your unwillingness to expose them to this test may raise the suspicion that you were unprepared.

7. Get Good Grades

In many courses class participation counts towards the final grade. Unwillingness to participate may lower your grade or even cause you to fail a course. Please note that this argument has been put as the last reason, not the first one, because the other reasons are better. It should not be a fear of failing that drives you to participate. It should be the joy of learning that pulls you.

After Class Reflection

It is extremely useful to have a short period of reflection right after class to evaluate your individual and small group preparation and large group participation against your understanding at the end of the class. Ask yourself, "What did I/we do right and why, and what did I/we miss and why?"

This critical reflection forms the basis for continuous self-improvement in your personal learning process. Too often, students charge out of class at the first opportunity without this quick reflection and lose the data necessary for continuous self- improvement.

CONCLUSION

Armed with the insights of the Case Difficulty Cube and the three stage case learning process, you are now ready to tackle the details of each of these stages. Thus, the next three chapters will provide further details, first, about individual preparation; second, about small group discussion; and third, about large group discussion.

individual preparation

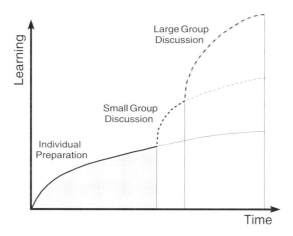

Sound individual preparation is the foundation of learning with cases and is the fundamental prerequisite for subsequent small and large group learning.

Preparing a case on your own is hard work. Cases can be long and complex, with or without assigned questions, and often do not have one or any "right answer." The open-ended nature of cases, the limited, or sometimes overwhelming, amount of information that is provided, and your inexperience with the issue, industry or product at stake can generate considerable confusion, frustration and even anxiety. Therefore, it is vital that you use your limited individual preparation time in a most effective manner. Individual preparation time usually ranges from one to two hours, depending on the case and related readings.

This chapter presents a disciplined and repeatable approach to individual preparation of a case. You will be introduced to the Short and Long Cycle Processes and the Case Preparation Chart as valuable major tools. Also discussed are: case assignments, the normal steps of the case solving process, immediate and basic issues in the case, the importance/urgency matrix, causes and effects, constraints and opportunities, decision criteria, quantitative and qualitative assessment, and missing information and assumptions. The chapter concludes with tips for effective individual preparation. If you are able to use these ideas effectively, you will have accomplished the largest single part of learning with cases.

CASE ASSIGNMENTS

If you are enrolled in a case course, you will usually receive an assignment prior to class which consists of a case to prepare and, possibly, other materials to read and understand. The order by which you decide to complete these two tasks may depend on the case or subject matter.

The Standard Assignment Question

"If you were in Tom Jones' position in this organization, what would be your analysis of the situation described, and what action would you take and why?" Case instructors use this standard type of assignment in a large variety of cases. And, if no assignment questions are provided, the student is supposed to ask him or herself a similar question.

For most participants, the first part of this standard assignment, "if you were in Tom Jones' position," is often the most challenging part of individual preparation in cases. You are expected to take the role of the focal person in the case. You do not need to change your own age or gender or personality or experience, but rather imagine yourself parachuted into the position currently occupied by Tom Jones. It is as if Tom Jones has suddenly left the organization and you have been asked to take his place. You bring your own values, age, gender, background, theoretical and practical understanding, training, expertise and culture into the position. The task facing Tom Jones has now become yours. The background to the organization and the issue remain as identified in the case, but the task is yours.

You may well ask, "Why is this so important? Who cares who owns the problem?" Actually, it is fundamental to the case learning process. Notice, the question is not, "If you were a consultant to Tom, what would you recommend?" Or, "Assess this organization's situation." Both of these latter approaches remove you at least one step from the role you are supposed to play. They change the case experience into a trip to the zoo. "Look at Tom Jones in his cage. How could he possibly get himself into a situation like that?" The case reader becomes a spectator, commentator or bystander but not a problem solver or decision maker.

Other Types of Assignments

Other types of assignments can also be given. Normally, these address specific course related concepts. Examples might be: "Please do a consumer analysis for tennis racquets. Draw a proposed organization chart. Prepare pro forma financial statements. Draw a process flow diagram." All are attempts by the instructor of the course to reinforce the value of certain tools or techniques or specific analyses. You should carry out such assigned tasks as requested.

Beyond the Assignment Questions

An unwritten rule in case preparation is that participants are expected to go beyond the assignment questions, if they have the time and the inclination. For example, a company may be in serious financial trouble and the introduction of a revolutionary new tennis racquet may not be financially possible. Or, at least, it should not be contemplated until the firm's financial troubles have been solved. Thus, a wonderful consumer analysis may very well identify a market niche perfectly suited to the new product design, a useful learning experience from a marketing perspective, but not the most pressing issue in this firm at this time. Even if the assignment question is focused on consumer analysis for this case, recognizing the financial realities would strengthen the analysis. Being able to prepare a case to address not only the specific assignment question(s) but also the implications beyond is a useful problem solving skill with high pay-offs.

There is an educational trap here. If the previously mentioned case was assigned by a marketing instructor with a specific consumer analysis assignment, it is advisable to complete the consumer analysis task rather than say, "This is totally meaningless since the company doesn't have the money to introduce this product anyway." Such shortcuts may not be perceived highly by the instructor, even though they may be perfectly logical in the context of the case.

THE SHORT CYCLE PROCESS

Most students new to learning with cases do not get started very well with case reading and preparation. They just start reading and re-reading and re-reading. Time slips away, frustration is overtaken by anxiety and general dissatisfaction prevails. We think there is a much better way to begin the individual preparation for every case, every time: the Short Cycle Process. Ideally this process should be completed the day before the Long Cycle Process and not exceed 15 minutes, regardless of the length or complexity of the case. It serves four purposes:

1. It quickly propels you inside the case.

2. It allows you to assess the case difficulty and the time required to complete the assignment.

3. It helps you determine whether or not you need extra help, i.e. to look at the theory, brush up on some analytical tools or do the readings before tackling the detailed analysis of the case.

4. It saves time by providing focus and direction to your subsequent detailed reading and analysis.

The Short Cycle Process has six steps (see Exhibit 3-1):

Step 1.   Read the first paragraph (or two or three) of the case and the last paragraph (or two or three) and stop to reflect.

Step 2.   Answer for yourself, preferably in summary form, the following five questions:

Who is the decision maker in the case that I am supposed to identify with and what position, title and responsibilities do I hold?

What appears to be my issue (concern, problem, challenge or opportunity) and its significance for the organization?

Why has my issue arisen and why am I involved now?

When do I have to decide, resolve, act or dispose of this issue? Is there an urgency?

How do I position this case on the Case Difficulty Cube? (See Chapter 2 for an explanation of The Case Difficulty Cube.)

Exhibit 3-1
INDIVIDUAL PREPARATION

I The Short Cycle Process

Purpose	Get a good feel or size-up for the case
Step 1	Read opening and ending paragraphs
Step 2	Who? What? Why? When? How?
Step 3	Quick look at the case exhibits
Step 4	Quick review of case subtitles
Step 5	Skim case body
Step 6	Read assignment questions and reflect

II The Long Cycle Process

Purpose	Analyze and solve the case
Part 1	Read the case
Part 2	Analyze the case
Step A	Define the issue
Step B	Analyze the case data
Step C	Generate alternatives
Step D	Select decision criteria
Step E	Assess alternatives
Step F	Select preferred alternative
Step G	Develop an action and implementation plan

If answers to these five questions are not revealed in reading these few paragraphs, keep a sharp eye in the subsequent steps. Sooner or later you will have to answer these questions if you are to have any confidence in your analysis. Typically, the expression "size-up of a case" can be equated to your answers to these questions.

Step 3. Turn to the exhibits, normally located at the end of the case, if there are any, read the titles and quickly survey the contents for initial impressions. For example, financial statements allow for a quick check of the financial health of the organization. An organization chart will help you see at a glance where you fit in the organization. You may see exhibits that are unique and perhaps confusing. The point here is that it is helpful just to get an overview of the scope and kind of material presented in the case.

Step 4. Review the headings as they appear in the body of the case for initial impressions. Following the opening paragraph(s), case information is normally organized under several headings ranging from the general to the more specific. Is the case well organized? Will you know where information is located for further reference? Will you have to do some of the organizing and searching yourself?

Step 5. Skim the body of the case quickly, perhaps by reading the first and last sentences of each paragraph. Now fill in the position on the presentation dimension of the Case Difficulty Cube in step 2 above.

Step 6. Read the assignment questions, if provided by your instructor, for special directions and reflect about how to approach the case.

At the end of this Short Cycle Process, you should have a solid perspective and sense of direction to pursue a more detailed analysis of the case. Fill in the top left side of the Case Preparation Chart (see Exhibit 3-2) to summarize your Short Cycle Process findings. It is useful to set the case aside for a while before proceeding with the Long Cycle Process.

THE LONG CYCLE PROCESS

The Long Cycle Process is composed of two major parts: 1) the detailed reading of the case and 2) the normal steps of the case solving process (see Exhibit 3-1).

Exhibit 3-2
CASE PREPARATION CHART

Case Title: *Case Assignment:*

I.   SHORT CYCLE PROCESS

       Name   Position

Who:

              Issue(s)
What:

Why:

When:

       Case Difficulty Cube

How: (_____, _____, _____)
       Analytical, Conceptual, Presentation

II.   LONG CYCLE PROCESS

   A.   Issue(s)

   Immediate   Basic

   1.   1.
   2.   2.
   3.   3.

   B.   Case Data Analysis

   (Apply course framework(s) and analytical tools.)

II.   LONG CYCLE PROCESS (continued)

   C.   Alternative Generation

      1.
      2.
      3.

   D.   Decision Criteria

      1.
      2.
      3.

   E.   Alternative Assessment

Quantitative	+			N			−		
Qualitative	+	N	−	+	N	−	+	N	−
Decision	go	go	?	?	no	no	?	no	no

   F.   Preferred Alternative

      Predicted Outcome

   G.   Action & Implementation Plan

                                    Timing
                                    Milestones
           Who
           What
           When
           Where
           How

      Missing Information

      Assumptions

Learning with Cases, 4th ed., Richard Ivey School of Business, 2007, p.36

Part 1: Detailed Reading of the Case

Armed with a solid initial perspective and focus, you are now ready to engage in part one of the Long Cycle Process of case preparation. This process starts with a careful and thoughtful reading of the case. Make notes in the margin or elsewhere to summarize ideas, raise questions, list particular concepts and record observations as they come to your mind.

Recognize that cases contain both facts and opinions. While you have to take facts at face value, you can certainly question or challenge opinions.

The case reading is not an "even paced, put equal emphasis on every word and figure" type of reading. Many, but not all, cases are organized in a typically predictable fashion as shown in Exhibit 3-3. We use this diagram to help train new case writers. It can assist you to determine where to spend most of your reading time.

Exhibit 3-3
NORMAL CASE OUTLINE

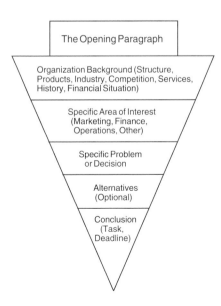

The Opening Paragraph

Typically, the opening paragraph provides a lens to the case. It identifies for the reader the name and location of the organization, who the decision maker is, what the decision or issue is and when the situation takes place.

Provided the case is written with a suitable opening paragraph, the key questions in the Short Cycle Process can all be answered by just reading the opening paragraph. Therefore, it requires extra special attention.

Organization Background Section

The next major portions of the case normally deal with the background of the organization as a whole and, possibly, the industry as well. This general background information can be voluminous, but not necessarily all relevant to the decision or issue identified in the opening paragraph. This section provides the context for the issue and it is there for a very important reason relating to contingency theory. It really is one of the prime reasons for using cases in the first place. Given that there are a variety of potential options in a decision, the preferred one "depends on the circumstances." If standard universal solutions existed, there would be no need for cases. If the answer for an investment decision is always "yes," then there is no need for deliberation. A parallel exists in medicine. Not every headache can be solved by taking one particular medicine. Thus, the doctor's analytical skills are required to distinguish between treatment options depending on the patient's personal health, age, economic, social and cultural factors.

On the whole, nevertheless, general background information can be read fairly quickly compared to other parts of the case.

The Specific Area of Interest

The general background section of the case is often followed by a more detailed description of the specific area in the organization in which the decision maker is employed. Thus, if this key person works in the human resources department, the case may provide further information about the functions of this department.

More information is also normally provided about the decision maker's position, job authority and responsibilities complemented, sometimes, with personal information about this key person. Notice that this section of the case is still background information and can be read fairly quickly.

The Specific Problem or Decision and Possible Alternatives

After all this contextual information cases provide further details about the issue referred to in the opening paragraph. Now you really slow down in your reading because these details become the most important and relevant information you will have to deal with.

If alternatives are provided in the case they tend to come next. These again require careful reading.

The Concluding Paragraph

Finally, the case will often contain a concluding paragraph or two which may also reinforce the time limit to which the person is working and restate the task. In essence the ending portion of the case takes the reader back to the opening paragraph and closes the loop.

Typical concluding statements are:

"Joan knew the committee would meet the following Wednesday and was expecting her recommendations then."

"The supplier had set a one month limit on this quotation."

"The marketing campaign would have to be fully planned at least three months before actual product introduction."

"The president said she would call back in one hour."

The concluding paragraph, therefore, may have significant impact on the urgency question which will be covered more fully later.

Exhibits

Many cases contain exhibits after the text portion of the case. Turn to the exhibits as they are referenced in the text to understand their context and content. Scrutinize them thoroughly. Some exhibits, such as financial statements or organization charts, may appear fairly standard. Still look for anything odd or unusual about them. Other exhibits are unique to the case and provide a summary or illustration of key data. Make sure that you understand the purpose of each exhibit.

Part 2: Analyze the Case

A generic approach to case analysis includes the following steps: A) define the issue; B) analyze the case data with focus on causes and effects as well as constraints and opportunities; C) generate alternatives; D) select decision criteria; E) assess alternatives; F) select the preferred alternative; and G) develop an action and implementation plan. Note that some parts of this model will not apply to every case and some aspects will receive more emphasis than others at different times during the course.

Specific analytical approaches, techniques and tools may be applied depending on the course, type of case and your instructor's particular requirements. It may be appropriate to re-visit regularly any particular analytical model, framework or concept suggested by your instructor or outlined in the course syllabus.

Step A. Define the Issue

Your initial job in case analysis is to develop a clear and comprehensive statement of the issue(s) involved in the case. The key concern(s), problem(s), decision(s), challenge(s) or opportunity(ies) you are facing as main actor of the case need to be clearly identified. The Short Cycle Process should have been very helpful in this first step.

The old adage, "stating the right problem takes you more than half way towards the right solution" certainly applies to case analysis. Unless you pose the right questions, you are unlikely to find the correct answers. This is why defining the issue(s) clearly is such a crucial part of your analysis. Do not be too hasty. What may appear to you as a problem may be only a symptom of a deeper hidden issue. Think of the tip of the iceberg phenomenon and get below the surface.

Immediate and Basic Issues. You will find that in almost all cases there are immediate as well as basic issues. The immediate issue refers to the specific decision, problem, challenge or opportunity faced by the decision maker in the case. For example, the decision focus may be on the purchase of software, where several options are available. The decision as to which of the software options to purchase is the immediate issue. Basic issues are larger and more generic in nature. They relate to the conceptual content and design of the course. For example, a basic issue in the software case might be "make or buy." Another could be the design of information systems. Yet another could be organizational roles and responsibilities: How much influence should the user of a software package have over this kind of purchase versus the chief information officer or the purchasing manager?

The immediate issue is the one that needs to be resolved within the time frame indicated in the case. Since few cases, if any, ever repeat themselves exactly in real life, the purpose of concerning yourself with the immediate issue is to develop a better grasp of the basic issue(s) underlying it. Basic issues tend to be ever present and common. Make or buy, information flow, and organizational roles and responsibilities issues occur in every organization all the time. The purchase of this particular package of software may never be faced by you in the future. Yet wrestling with it and dealing with the details appropriately is a valuable aid in developing an approach generalizable to a host of other situations.

Importance. One of the first judgements that needs to be made about the case issue is whether this issue is of strategic importance to the organization or not. Could it make or break the organization? Could it be a source of major competitive advantage? Could it impact the profitability significantly? Could it have a major effect on the morale of the employees or on the corporate image?

Urgency. As part of the first step of defining the issue, a feeling for the sense of urgency is fundamental to effective case analysis. A good analogy is the emergency room in a hospital. Someone comes in and the attendant behind the counter makes a very quick judgment whether this patient can go through the regular routine process of registration and sit in the waiting room until his or her turn, or whether the patient needs to be brought directly in for immediate attention. The same feel for timing must be developed with cases. Is this decision critical and everything has to be dropped to tend to it or can it wait for some time?

The combination of importance and urgency places the case issue on a priority list and will affect the criteria for decision making, the resources that should be used, including the amount of money that can be spent, and the options which may be considered to resolve it. That is why putting the issue in context early is vital to effective case analysis.

A simple 2-by-2 matrix highlights the potential combinations of importance and urgency (see Exhibit 3-4).

Exhibit 3-4
CASE ISSUE IMPORTANCE AND URGENCY MATRIX

IMPORTANCE ⟋ URGENCY	LOW	HIGH
LOW	I	II
HIGH	III	IV

Quadrant IV represents both high importance and high urgency requiring quick action on a critical issue. In contrast, Quadrant I represents a minor issue without much urgency which can be resolved eventually. It is good practice in case analysis to place the key case issue on this importance/urgency matrix and, therefore, a provision for this has been made in Exhibit 3-2, the Case Preparation Chart.

Step B. Analyze the Case Data

It is not possible to use this little corner of the Case Preparation Chart to summarize your analysis of the case data. Therefore, it is necessary to go off the chart and use as many pages as your need for this task. Proper analysis is vital before alternatives and decision criteria can be assessed and should not be rushed. Usually a significant amount of individual preparation, small group and large group discussion time is spent on case analysis to ensure the correct interpretation of relevant case data has been achieved. If you are interested in obtaining high grades in a case course, case analysis provides a wonderful opportunity to distinguish yourself.

Case analysis has to be pursued from a course as well as a decision making context. Your instructor will provide the analytical tools and theories from a course perspective. This text addresses only the decision making or problem solving framework.

Every course you take will have its own body of knowledge and theoretical framework including concepts, tools, techniques and practices pertaining to the field of study. Normally this material is available in a textbook, course notes, library and internet references. Therefore, while this book reinforces the decision framework in a neutral sense, the other course materials aid in providing supporting tools for decision making in a particular context. For example, in marketing, consumer analysis is a vital analytical tool in a large range of marketing decisions. In finance, the ability to read and interpret financial statements is a core competency required in finance related decisions.

Your instructor in your course will identify the major course specific analytical and theoretical approaches which will assist you in properly analyzing situations, opportunities, challenges, decisions and problems related to the course focus. When analyzing a case you are expected to demonstrate your understanding of the field by the appropriate application of course related theories, concepts and tools to the specific decision in the case.

A major objective of the case method is to develop your ability to connect appropriately the "wisdom of the field" to the particular decision at hand. Thus, while many cases can be analyzed from a "common sense" perspective, it is the field related skills and understanding that should distinguish professional from novice analysis. An obvious parallel exists in the medical profession which recognizes the difference in analytical and execution skills between the general practitioner and the heart transplant surgeon.

The problem solving aspect of case analysis is often concerned with causes and effects.

Causes and Effects. Problems cannot be solved unless their causes have been identified. Establishing the causes of problems is not always easy and may require you to think about relationships between events as well as between people to sort out causes from effects.

The challenge in analyzing the causal sequences of events is to separate causes from effects and to try to work backward to determine what may be the "root" causes.

Constraints and Opportunities. You should also identify constraints or opportunities which will impact on your analysis and ultimately on your recommendations. Constraints and opportunities are not always explicit in the case, although they may be implied by the environmental context, or the date and location of the case.

Consider the key resources of an organization to be money, people, materials, equipment, facilities and the management system. Each of these resources or a combination of them can be a constraint or an opportunity.

Quantitative and Qualitative Analysis. Almost every case has quantitative as well as qualitative dimensions. Frequently, students prefer the qualitative over the quantitative. Please try to avoid this inclination. Push the numbers, play with the numbers and you may get a much better feel for the whole situation. The use of computers has made the pushing of numbers relatively easy. One has to be careful however not to get lost in detailed numerical analysis with little reflection about what these numbers actually mean.

Figuring out which calculations to do is challenging for most students. Prof. D. Maister from the Harvard Business School, who thinks that the ability to do numbers is not innate but rather a matter of approach, offers some useful suggestions that we have summarized below:

- Take it slowly.
- Always know why you are doing a calculation, what you intend to do with the result, and how you plan to interpret it.
- Train your business intuition by guessing at the answer before you perform the calculation.
- Break your calculations down into their various steps clearly on paper.
- Write down all calculations as if they were going to be read by someone else.
- Always identify the units or dimensions of every number you write down. Confusion over units is a primary source of errors.
- Make liberal use of your visual sense when searching for numerical meaning. Draw a graph or a diagram to facilitate your interpretation.
- Carefully reassemble and review your various calculations. A number only has meaning when compared with another, such as a standard, past experience, expectation or another number in the case (Maister 1-4).

Step C. Generate Alternatives

The next part of the case solving process deals with trying to remove the cause(s) of the problem(s) by developing a number of different ways to address the issue(s) of the case. Now is the time to be creative and think widely. If an alternative is not part of the original set which will be analyzed, all further work on the decision will ignore the missed alternative's potential.

When you are formulating different alternatives, consider constraints and opportunities that you have identified in the preceding data analysis phase. Refer to your own knowledge or past experience as well as to any theory gleaned from your readings. Make your alternatives realistic and plausible in view of your causal analysis and understanding of the issue(s).

It has been suggested that better managers tend to generate more alternatives. If the case already contains one or more alternatives, look for at least one new one. Simple alternatives include doing something or doing nothing, spending money or not spending it; or similar opposites like make or buy, hire or do not hire, invest or divest, retain or dismiss, introduce or withdraw, increase or decrease. By the way, the status quo can almost always be considered as an alternative. Doing nothing has at least one advantage, ease of implementation. You can also consider combining alternatives.

Step D. Select Decision Criteria

Before choosing one or a combination of your alternatives, it is important that you clearly define the criteria against which to compare all possible alternatives. Decision criteria provide the basis for evaluation or assessment measures. They are the standards by which alternatives may be evaluated and compared.

Decision criteria can be classified as quantitative as well as qualitative. Exhibit 3-6 gives a list of frequently used criteria. This list of criteria is not exhaustive and, under certain circumstances, items listed under the left hand column of Exhibit 3-6 might well move to the right and vice versa. Ease of measurement and quantification under the circumstances of the specific case being analyzed will determine whether the criterion is qualitative or quantitative.

Exhibit 3-6
LIST OF COMMON DECISION CRITERIA

QUANTITATIVE	QUALITATIVE
profit	competitive advantage
cost	customer satisfaction
return on investment	employee morale
market share	corporate image
capacity	ease of implementation
delivery time	synergy
risk	ethics
cash flow	flexibility
inventory turn	safety
productivity	visual appeal
staff turnover	obsolescence
quality	cultural sensitivity
growth rate	motivation
quantity	goodwill

In your selection of the most appropriate criteria for each case, you should be guided by what you believe are the objectives or strategy of the organization and by your good sense of what is important to you as the decision maker. Keeping in mind that your future career might well be riding on the quality of your decision can help make criteria selection as realistic as possible.

Step E. Assess Alternatives

A standard way to compare alternatives is to list the key advantages and disadvantages of each alternative. Only after generating the list should you attempt to weigh these pros and cons to select the best course of action.

You need to compare and contrast each of your alternatives against the criteria you have selected, in order to make the best decision. To help your assessment and comparison of alternatives, you may wish to use a matrix such as the example provided in Exhibit 3-7. Even if you do not have precise data to fill in the matrix, it is still advisable to use a ranking system. For example, highest, medium, or lowest customer satisfaction and shortest to longest delivery time are ways to rank alternatives.

Exhibit 3-7
ALTERNATIVE ASSESSMENT MATRIX

Alternatives	Decision Criteria			
	Cost	Time	Ease of Implementation	Customer Satisfaction
1.				
2.				
3.				
4.				

Even if you find completing the information in the above matrix mostly straight forward, making the final decision can still be quite challenging. Whenever multiple decision criteria need to be applied, the weighting of each criterion versus the others has to be decided. In the example in Exhibit 3-7, one person might give cost a 70% weighting and each of the others 10%. Someone else might put customer satisfaction as the highest rating and end up preferring another alternative.

Short versus Long Term. In almost every case, concerns about the short and the long term exist. In assessing alternatives, predicting outcomes, as well as planning and implementing action, both short and long term considerations are relevant. Which is preferable: (1) An alternative that has quick highly beneficial results and mediocre long term ones or (2) an alternative with good long term prospects but no immediate pay-offs? What actions need to be taken in the short term and what additional ones in the long term?

Moreover, what is short-term and what is long-term? In highly urgent situations, short-term might be defined in terms of minutes, hours or days; and long-term as days or weeks. In less urgent situations, short-term might be weeks or months; and long-term years.

It is the continuing exercise of judgment based on the case situation and your experience that makes case learning such a unique endeavor.

Predicting Outcomes. Most cases deal with situations or decisions involving a change in the organization. For example, the case may deal with an investment proposal. Is it worthwhile to invest money in this proposal? Clearly, the future benefits expected from the investment have to justify spending the money now. Prediction of future results and consequences of any change is a fundamental step in alternative assessment.

The issue of uncertainty arises with any prediction and forces you to assess probabilities for various random events which may impact the outcomes. A decision tree diagram is a useful tool for visualizing and quantifying options and alternatives. Where considerable uncertainty exists regarding future outcomes, it is useful to forecast the best, worst, and most likely outcomes (see Exhibit 3-8).

Exhibit 3-8
SIMPLIFIED DECISION TREE DIAGRAM

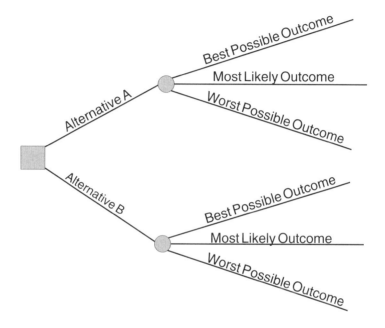

Quantitative versus Qualitative Assessment. Almost every case alternative may be evaluated on both quantitative and qualitative factors by ranking each as positive (+), neutral (N) or negative (-). If the quantitative (including the financial) side suggests that a particular idea is positive, then the qualitative side does not have to support the proposition strongly. Exhibit 3-9 shows the relation between the quantitative side and the qualitative aspects of the alternative analysis.

Thinking of alternatives in this context allows you to guide your decision in the right direction and also to identify where judgment becomes most difficult. You can see that a proposal that is attractive quantitatively as well as qualitatively comes to an easy "go" decision. The tough decisions are the question marks which occur only in three out of the nine possible combinations. In each of these three situations judgment is required to determine where the balance should lie between the quantitative and the qualitative factors.

Exhibit 3-9
QUANTITATIVE AND QUALITATIVE
ALTERNATIVE ASSESSMENT

Quantitative	+			N			−		
Qualitative	+	N	−	+	N	−	+	N	−
Decision	go	go	?	?	no	no	?	no	no

The Case Preparation Chart (Exhibit 3-2) provides this matrix on which you can mark your assessment of the alternative as positive, neutral or negative; and the consequent "go", "question mark" or "no go" decision. This quick perspective indicates your assessment as to why action should be taken. A question mark conclusion tends to suggest that a decision is not all that obvious and that quality of argument may swing the decision one way or another.

Step F. Select Preferred Alternative

The ultimate point in case analysis is to address the issue(s) presented and to make a decision. If you have done a good job at predicting outcomes and comparing alternatives, the course of action which best meets your objectives may be obvious.

Decision making is not always so simple, however, if you are faced with several issues combined with multiple objectives and decision criteria. There is rarely only one sensible course of action to a case. It is your analysis, the use you make of the information available, and your justification for adopting a certain alternative that counts. What you are trying to create is a path to the answer. Therefore, you could recommend a perfectly good solution, but receive a poor grade because your reasoning is not consistent with the solution recommended. For example, you would not be consistent if you argue that the purchase of a $9,000 piece of equipment is not worth getting the whole organization upset about, and then recommend writing a ten page report with copies to the vice-president manufacturing and all the other bosses in the company about your opposition to this purchase.

Step G. Develop an Action and Implementation Plan

After making the best decision you must now develop an action and implementation plan. Even though this step of the case solving model is crucial, it often gets neglected. Sometimes in your own preparation you will run out of time and not give action planning the attention it deserves. Often the large group discussion runs out of time and overlooks this phase. Furthermore, it is difficult to decide on the level of detail necessary to develop a good plan. There is no doubt, nonetheless, that your skill in developing a sound action and implementation plan will prepare you well for the future.

To guide you in this part of the case solving model, you can refer back to your analysis and focus your attention on specifying the actions necessary to produce the advantages (pros) and avoid or minimize the disadvantages (cons) that you have identified earlier.

Your action plan must be specific and answer five basic questions: who, what, when, where and how? Moreover, a useful addition is a contingency plan in case things do not go as expected.

Most students and in fact many managers are not very skillful in formulating well developed action plans. One secret is to practise continuously the 1/3-2/3 rule of action planning. The 1/3-2/3 rule says that the first 1/3 of your action plan should contain 2/3 of the specific steps about who, what, when, where and how. Misplaced concreteness occurs when five year projections are calculated to three decimals while the decision-maker has neglected to specify the first three action steps that need to be taken.

Planning the Implementation. It is often said that managers do not fail to analyze and decide but often fail to implement their decision. And it is equally often said that people do not do what they said they would do. Implementation planning provides a schedule and milestones for the action plan. It provides the measures or signals that will allow managers to know they are making progress according to plan.

Remember that ease of implementation of a decision is in itself a criterion for alternative selection, as seen in the selecting decision criteria phase of this process. Therefore, implementation needs to be considered before the alternative selection is made.

Developing the action and implementation plan completes the Long Cycle Process. Nevertheless, in each of the seven steps in the Long Cycle Process you may lack sufficient information and be forced to make assumptions.

Missing Information and Assumptions

Your analysis should be based for the most part on the information available in the case. We say for the most part because you can use your own background and experience to provide the political, economical, social, and technological context of the case.

At times, you may feel that you do not have enough information to assess the situation. This is a reflection of reality. Most managers do not possess all the information either, or are not able to acquire it, before making decisions.

If you think you need more information, be prepared to answer the following five questions:

1. What information do I really need to have?
2. Why do I think it is critical to have this information?
3. Where do I think this information is located? Who has it?
4. How much time and money will it take to produce it?
5. If provided, what difference will it make to my decision?

Routinely, managers are forced to make decisions based on partial information and, of necessity, make assumptions. You will have ample opportunity to develop your skills in making sound assumptions.

Making assumptions can be a delicate matter. The obvious danger lies in creating fiction that bears little resemblance to the case at hand. You should recognize when you are making an assumption and you should be prepared to justify it. Explain the rationale for your assumption, the evidence, knowledge or experience you base it on. Be careful of hidden assumptions — those you have made implicitly or without awareness. Your assumptions should be plausible, realistic, and helpful in the light of the circumstances of the case. You need to make sensible inferences tied to known facts.

Various kinds of assumption may require different treatment. Five common types are:

1. *Context Assumption.* For example, if the case tells you only that you are a buyer for a large corporation, it is safe to assume that the purchasing department will be reasonably large, not a one person operation, and that you most likely report to a purchasing manager. Generally speaking, this kind of assumption does not need to be written down or discussed in your case analysis, because it is considered obvious.

2. *"Normal State of Affairs"* Assumption. There is a whole class
    of assumptions that we might call "normal state of affairs"
    or "reasonableness" assumptions based on trust in the case
    writer. Unless the case writer has indicated otherwise, we
    presume the normal state of affairs holds. For example, if it
    is not explicitly stated that the company or organization is
    in dire financial straits, we can reasonably assume it is in a
    satisfactory financial position.

3. *Decision Criterion Assumption.* If the decision you are
    considering is the lease or purchase of a steam generator,
    the assumption of a two to three year payback period may
    be called a decision criterion assumption. Obviously, it is
    important to identify clearly this type of assumption
    because it impacts on the solution to the case.

4. *If-Then Assumption.* This assumption goes like this: "If I do
    this, then this is likely to follow." This kind of assumption,
    often used in the selection of the best course of action or in
    the implementation phases, is the most touchy because it
    allows you to assume the whole problem away. It is
    necessary to argue both sides of the fence. "If it works —
    fine; if not, then something else would be done next."

5. *The "Perfect Person" Assumption.* Probably the most
    dangerous and least useful assumption in all cases is the
    "perfect person" assumption. "I will get rid of the current
    manager and hire the 'perfect person' who will solve this
    situation successfully" or "I will hire the best consultant
    and this consultant will give me the perfect solution" are
    two illustrations of this type of assumption.

Evaluating Results

Normally, for most cases, evaluation of results, the last step
mentioned in most problem solving models, does not apply
during the individual preparation process. Therefore, the
individual case preparation ends with the identification of the

preferred alternative with the expected outcome and the specification of the action and implementation plan.

In real life, this last phase of evaluating results takes place some time after completing the implementation. Managers are then in a position to evaluate how well their decision(s) has contributed to the performance measures used in the organization and whether the predicted outcomes have really materialized.

With respect to your own learning with cases, you may ask yourself, "When and how do I get the chance to evaluate the results of decisions?" Recall the first degree on the case analytical dimension: the problem or issue is stated and the solution or decision taken by the manager is given (see Chapter 2). Your key task in such a case is to evaluate the quality of the decision. Was it implemented carefully? Were the best alternatives identified and analyzed? Were the causes of the problem identified properly? In essence, you are asked to start at the end of the problem solving process and work backwards through the various steps in making your evaluation of the quality of the decision making process.

In some instances you may be introduced to the series type of case. These are cases that have (A), (B), (C) and (D) parts for example. Instructors hand out one part at a time and you are encouraged to evaluate what happened and why.

Moreover, in the reflection periods after small and large group discussions you get a chance to review your own decisions and your preparation process against the collective wisdom of the small and large groups.

TIPS FOR EFFECTIVE INDIVIDUAL PREPARATION

The individual preparation task is a complex one as the previous pages indicate. There are a number of ways in which you can increase your effectiveness in preparing quickly and well. Following is a list of practical tips to save time and enhance the quality of your individual preparation.

- Do not read the case over and over again. Do not try to memorize case facts. Always start with the "Short Cycle Process" (Exhibit 3-1) and use the Case Preparation Chart (Exhibit 3-2) to guide and summarize your work.

- Read and prepare during the time of day when your personal effectiveness is high. Some students are morning people; others shine at night. It will help shorten the total time required if you prepare at the right time of day.

- Block uninterrupted regular periods of time. Do not think in terms of three or four hour time blocks. Rather, focus your attention for short time periods, even 15 to 20 minute blocks. Make sure to take a break after every one to one and a half hours.

- Follow the principle that scheduled activities take precedence over unscheduled ones. Write down your case preparation commitments and do not let other activities or people steal your time.

- Read and prepare during times when you can combine this activity with others; for example, on the bus while you are travelling, or while eating.

- Set a time limit for yourself and really try to stick to it. If you let the case analysis process take its natural course without time restriction, it may never get completed.

- There is no need to do all the preparation at once. Separate the "Short Cycle Process" from the "Long Cycle Process" to allow for some reflection and more objectivity.

- If you have more than one case to prepare, consider combining your Short Cycle Process preparations for several cases.

- Consider doing your additional reading, if assigned, before starting your case analysis. It may provide clues to relevant themes, concepts, tools and practices in the field, and therefore help your case preparation.

- When you are frustrated because you cannot seem to get into the case, have a five-minute hot-line telephone call with a classmate: "Frank, I'm having trouble getting into the Dynatex case. What are you doing about it?... Thanks. I'll see you tomorrow. Bye." Try it.

- If you find yourself getting lost in the numbers, revisit Maister's tips.

- Find yourself an effective work place.

THE CASE PREPARATION CHART

To wrap up your individual preparation, use the Case Preparation Chart (see Exhibit 3-2). This chart starts with the Short Cycle Process on the top left hand side and evolves on the right hand side to the decision, action and implementation plan. Note that sections E, F, and G refer only to the preferred alternative. An enlargement of this chart will provide a convenient overview of your individual preparation. It does have to be supplemented by additional pages of calculations and analytical work. Each course has its own framework for case analysis which needs to be reflected in your notes and case preparation. The Case Preparation Chart is intended to be a generic aid to individual preparation and note taking. It is a guide and road map to effective case preparation. It leads you through a logical series of steps which allow you to focus your efforts on the content of case preparation and minimize your concerns about the process. The content of your preparation is your responsibility. It is not the purpose of this book to supply the content learning you will get in each course you take. And the Case Preparation Chart will be highly useful in your small group as well as large group discussions, the next two phases of learning with cases.

small group discussion

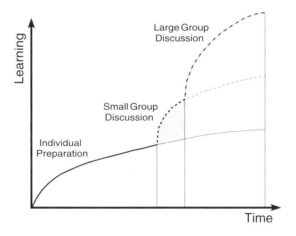

The small group discussion, the second step of the three stage case learning process, provides the vital link between individual preparation and large group (or class) discussion. Small groups, which may also be referred to as study groups, learning teams, syndicates, or break-out groups, give every member an opportunity to discuss his or her insights to the case.

This process is often reflected in real life public and private spheres, when large group meetings are conducted after the business at hand has been discussed by smaller units such as project teams, task forces or committees.

Why a whole chapter on this subject? Who has the time for small group discussion? If you have done the individual preparation thoroughly, can you not skip this step? We believe that the small group discussion forms a vital part of your preparation task. Collective effort will surpass individual preparation. The purpose of the small group is not to duplicate your individual preparation or class discussion but, as illustrated in the above diagram, to provide an opportunity to increase your performance, to push you up to a higher level of learning. Moreover, these small group working sessions, when properly executed, constitute an enriching part of the whole case learning experience.

The reasons for having a small group discussion on each case, faithfully, case after case, have already been provided in Chapter 2. Now the focus will be on small group effectiveness. What should you bring to the group and what can you take away from it? How can you make sure your small group is functioning well and productively? The first task is organizing for effective small group work.

ORGANIZING FOR EFFECTIVE SMALL GROUP WORK

Most institutions rarely force students to work in small groups and few provide mechanisms to organize them formally. You are often left largely on your own for this task. Whether or not your institution promotes or facilitates regular small group work, we invite you to take the initiative and assume the responsibility to form your own.

Size

To maximize the benefits of a small group, your group should have a minimum of three and a maximum of five members. Larger than five, the opportunity for individual members to participate and contribute to the group diminishes, with a resulting loss of productivity for the group and satisfaction for each member. In a 20 minute small group discussion, three members can have 6.7 minutes of talking time each; six members would only have 3.3 minutes, a 50% reduction.

Composition

Considerable attention should be devoted to the composition of your group. Basing your group selection strictly on past friendships or geographic considerations could be quite limiting. Ideally, your group should reflect a variety of skills, cultures, experiences and expertise. Your discussion will be enriched by the variety of perspectives from members with diverse backgrounds. A balance of quantitatively and qualitatively oriented people is bound to increase the overall learning in the group discussions.

Just as important as the mix of talents will be the personal willingness and commitment of prospective members to work cooperatively and assiduously. Sharing the same values regarding the importance of small groups and the usefulness of proper individual preparation will prevent a lot of conflicts.

How do you find out about your classmates' talents? How do you assess their compatibility and reliability? This can take time and the institution can play a role that will help in this respect.

Rotation

In some schools, small groups start off on some forced rotation basis for the first few weeks. Only after this exposure to classmates do students choose their own group. Some four or five weeks later, it is possible to unfreeze these groups and allow groups to go into a rotation again for a week or two and then reform. In executive programs, the small groups are often mixed on a regular basis to allow exposure to fellow class members.

If your institution is not formally involved in small group formation, you may tell prospective members that it is for a fixed try-out period only. It is desirable to schedule a review of your group composition after some experience with each other has accumulated. Logical times for such a review could be mid-term or after exams.

Time

Time devoted to the small group discussion is related to the size of your group. The more members you have, the more time your small group will likely take. Twenty to thirty minutes per case will normally be sufficient, assuming a group of three to five persons and solid individual preparation prior to the small group discussion.

Students often complain that small group discussions take too much time. The most common time-waster is the deterioration of the group into a working session. Once a small group starts doing a joint case analysis and action plan, it becomes a lengthy proposition. The slowest member of the group sets the pace. It is essential that you keep reminding yourself that the small group is not a crutch for poor individual preparation, but a tool to achieve a higher level of learning.

Some students combine their small group discussions, that is, they discuss more than one case in one sitting. This practice, of course, requires a fair amount of planning but it is worth the effort.

Our main message here is that you have to manage and contain this small group process or it will consume you. We are not trying to create workaholics. Quite the opposite, we are trying to save time while maximizing your learning. Your aim should simply be to do as good a job as possible in the small group within the time available.

Timing

Find a time for your meetings that makes it as convenient as possible for everyone to get together. Sometimes factors beyond your control make it difficult to have small group discussions. An evening adult class where participants come from all over town is a typical example of such a situation. While not ideal, you may be able to persuade your group members to arrive early and have your meetings half an hour before class.

Ideally, the small group discussion should take place close enough to the large group discussion that the acquired learning remains fresh in your memory but not so close as to prevent you from reflecting and pondering how you will translate your added learning into class contribution.

Location

Some students meet at home; others at school. Some rotate the place where they meet. Many institutions provide small rooms which may be booked ahead of time. It does not really matter where you meet as long as it is consistent, convenient and conducive to work. The bar across from the campus will not fit all three criteria, obviously.

Some small groups make use of the phone through teleconferencing. This medium, while not ideal because it cuts you off from all the non-verbal aspects of communication, at least forces you to be disciplined in your use of time. Face to face communication is certainly preferable.

ESTABLISHING SMALL GROUP GUIDELINES

Every small group develops its own rules of conduct, standards of participation, and expectations of how members should behave. To increase discussion process effectiveness, we suggest you adopt the following guidelines for standard day-to-day case preparation.

1. *Each individual must attend the small group discussion and must be fully prepared.* Each group member has honestly tried his or her best to prepare as well as possible within the individual preparation time available ahead of time. There should be no one ill-prepared and just sponging off the group. The small group is definitely not the place to start your individual preparation.

2. *Each member of the group must participate actively in the small group discussion.* Each member agrees to share his or her key ideas and insights which then become communal property. The climate is clearly one of collaboration, not competition. You should be concerned about the learning of the other members as well as your own. Under this guideline, it is perfectly acceptable to bring into the classroom the points that you acquired in the small group. However, your colleagues will always appreciate it if you recognize their special contributions in class.

3. *It is not necessary to have a small group leader, in the sense of decision maker.* Each person must reach his or her own decisions based on the small group discussion as well as the individual preparation. Having a facilitator to keep the group on track, make sure everybody participates and manage the time available is entirely appropriate, however.

4. *It is not necessary to have a small group recording secretary.* Each individual is responsible for his or her own notes. Recognizing good ideas when they are offered is a skill worth practicing by all members. Use of the Case Preparation Chart (Exhibit 3-2) for your own note-taking is highly recommended.

5. *Appointing a small group spokesperson is not required.* Everyone will speak for him or herself in the classroom. (Sometimes, instructors give special assignments to groups which require the appointment of a spokesperson. This is

not the type of small group we are referring to in this chapter. Chapter 6 will cover small group presentations.)

6. *Achieving consensus or a "group position" is normally not necessary.* You do not have to agree with each other with respect to the solution of the case. In real life, consensus is important so that major decisions can be implemented with the support of key stakeholders. In small group discussion about cases, diversity of opinions and options enriches the learning process and there is insufficient time available to achieve consensus.

7. *Establish and stick to the time limit.* A good rule of thumb should be no more than thirty minutes of small group time for a normal case. Depending on the size of the group and the type of case, it could be as short as twenty minutes.

Some people may argue that this short period of time only promotes skimming of the case. Actually, a lot can be accomplished in twenty to thirty minutes provided that you and your teammates come fully prepared. The small group is not the place to start a joint case analysis.

DISCUSSING IN THE SMALL GROUP

How does the small group work? How do you get the best out of your group? What happens during the small group discussion? It is important to establish a routine and stick to it. The following agenda works well for your discussion using your Case Preparation Chart.

1. **Quick review of the Short Cycle Process conclusions.** Do all members agree as to what the issue(s) of this case is and from which viewpoint it must be addressed? Please note that the consensus you should achieve here is about issue definition, not about solution(s).

2. **Review of the Long Cycle Process conclusions.** Everyone in the group contributes his or her analysis and solution if it is different from what has been discussed so far. Discussing key conclusions from the Long Cycle Process is where practice for class occurs and where you should spend the bulk of your small group time.

3. **Review of special difficulties.** Having group members talk about special difficulties with either the interpretation of facts, the analysis, the process or something else, provides golden opportunities for you to learn by teaching. If the help that someone may require at this point is beyond the scope of the time limit for this part of the small group discussion, identifying where this help will come from and when can always be arranged.

4. **Anticipation of the class discussion.** If time permits, a good way to conclude the discussion is to share any insights as to what may happen in class: where the emphasis of the large group discussion may be placed; how the instructor may attack it; what could be the leading questions; or how does this case fit into the course design. This last part of the small group discussion should assist you with the final phase of your preparation, your class contribution agenda, which is discussed at the end of this chapter.

IDENTIFYING SMALL GROUP PROBLEMS

"Freud...was right about human groups: They bring out the best and the worst of the species. At best, groups are superior to individuals because they can accomplish more work, are more creative, have more information, and offer more pleasure through the process of task accomplishment. At worst, groups waste time insidiously, accomplish little work, and create an arena in which interpersonal conflict can rage" (Vance 217). A certain degree of conflict within a group is not necessarily bad, however. It can be the characteristic of high performance. It can make for lively exchange of ideas and stimulate creative thinking. Some types of misbehavior can easily creep into small groups, nonetheless, and should be dealt with because such behaviors can result in serious interpersonal conflicts and be highly dysfunctional.

   In order to address such dysfunctional behaviors and devise strategies for handling the conflicts, it may be useful to identify some common types of problems. These problems may belong to four categories: (1) time mismanagement, (2) lack of preparation, (3) interpersonal problems, and (4) lack of commitment. Obviously, they do not cover everything that can go wrong in a small group discussion.

1. **Time mismanagement.** The small group discussion consumes too much time. The small group has an inability to set and stick to a time limit. Sometimes the small group rehashes case facts, gets off topic or lacks facilitation skills in its membership to keep the process in check.

2. **Lack of preparation.** All or some small group members do not come fully prepared to contribute to the small group discussion. Sometimes, members will put in only a "satisficing" performance; not the best one they can do but just enough to get by.

3. **Interpersonal problems.** Following is a list of some of the most common behavioral problems that may affect one or more persons in the group and lead to conflicts with the other small group members.

   Apathy: passivity, lack of involvement, unjustified absence, low participation, or over-dependence on others.

   Attacking: name-calling, berating, belittling the competence of another.

   In-fighting: constantly arguing, working in a competitive mode as opposed to a cooperative one.

Dominating: ordering, taking charge, bullying, interrupting, cutting off, insisting on getting one's own way; and exerting social pressure on others, which may lead to conformity of thought and suppression of creativity.

Horseplaying: taking the group away from its task by engaging in unrelated activities, fooling around, making disruptive jokes. By the way, we certainly do not mean to discourage mixing fun with learning. A certain amount of humor can be a key ingredient in group cohesiveness and satisfaction.

Blocking: slowing progress by repeatedly raising objections, constantly bringing up the same topic after it has been addressed by the group, sabotaging the process.

Resenting: sarcasms, aggressiveness, harboring feelings of rancor, bitterness or frustration because one group member may, for example, feel he or she is working harder than other members who are getting better results.

Whining: always complaining, criticizing, looking at the negative side of things.

4. **Lack of commitment.** If the small group is not fully committed to the small group discussion stage of the learning process and adequate individual preparation beforehand, it may provoke a chain reaction involving all three previous categories of problems.

Dealing with Small Group Problems

In our opinion, the best way to deal with all categories of small group problems is to strive to create a learning environment which discourages the emergence of these troublesome group or individual behaviors. You should focus on preventing such problems and on minimizing their negative impact on the group, if they do appear.

Here are some suggestions:

1. Set some regular times to review the process of your small group meetings. Allow for open debriefing of your sessions. "How are we doing? Are there any suggestions for improvement?" are useful questions to raise periodically.

2. Revisit and discuss the norms and guidelines on how your group operates. Try to obtain consensus.

3. Do not tolerate misbehavior. Before a pattern is established, confront it in an assertive manner. Do not blame, threaten, or blow up. Calmly, using "I" statements, express your objection to the behavior and explain why you object to it.

4. Vent your feelings regularly, do not let frustration accumulate. Something small may get out of perspective. Iron out minor disagreements between individuals after and not during the small group discussion itself.

5. Do not assume sole responsibility for the performance of the whole group. If you see that you are the only one doing proper individual preparation and cannot get your group to change, break from the group and search for another one that shares your values.

6. Adopt an open, receptive, and tolerant attitude. Try to understand the root of the issue. Does it stem from cultural differences, conflicting values? Is it possible that the problem is with you because you are prejudiced against certain people?

7. Literally, address the problem as your own live case. Apply the case solving model.

8. Get external advice if the conflict escalates beyond the

point that you can address it within the group. Some institutions have counselors and special advisors who are used to dealing with this type of problem. They may agree to have a private talk with a disruptive member or talk with the group as a whole.

9. If no change in behavior occurs and it becomes truly unbearable, ask the troublesome character to leave the group. Sometimes, people are truly incompatible and a no blame, amicable divorce is the best solution. However, learning to deal with difficult persons is a skill that may serve you well in your future career.

In summary, please realize that conflicts do occur, that these are not always negative, that prevention and early detection are the best remedies and, finally, that they may give you the opportunity to further practice problem solving in a real time, real life mode.

To end this rather negative section on a positive note, it is useful to recognize that it is great to be on a winning team. Success breeds success. Good individual preparation and small group discussion bring positive results in the classroom and on reports and exams. Rejoice as a group in your accomplishments. A little bit of praise for each other goes a lot farther than chronic whining. Support your small group members not only in academic matters but also personal ones. The team will find working hard and playing hard tremendously satisfying.

REFLECTING ON THE SMALL GROUP AND PREPARING YOUR CLASS CONTRIBUTION AGENDA

Your preparation task does not end with a successfully completed individual case analysis and effective small group discussion. Before moving into the classroom, it is important that you spend some time to assimilate the new learning that occurred in the small group. This reflection period or "soak time" will be beneficial to the extent that you are willing to articulate the new learning and integrate it to your prior individual preparation.

Be aware that the best case preparation will not necessarily translate into star performance in the classroom unless you prepare your contribution to the large group discussion. You now have to direct your attention to the presentation of your case analysis, to the communication of your ideas. The focus moves to planning your contribution to the class. This task is complicated because you do not know when or even if you will be asked to contribute. Therefore, contributions can seldom be planned in detail and executed as planned. "By the very nature of the classroom situation, decisions regarding 'what to say' and 'how to say it' will be made on the spot in the classroom" (Easton 186). Nevertheless, here are some suggestions that will help you prepare your points and help ensure that they are well received.

1. Update your Case Preparation Chart. This summary chart (Exhibit 3-2) will be your best tool, as it will help you to stay focused.

2. Organize any other notes. Know where everything is. If your instructor follows a predictable discussion structure, then you may wish to organize your material accordingly. Material organization will prevent you from getting lost in a sea of details if asked a specific question.

3. Try to anticipate some unassigned questions pertaining to the case that the instructor may ask.

4. Do not try to memorize or rehearse a set presentation. It is difficult to present long and complex arguments without being interrupted by your classmates who also want to make their own points. Rather be prepared to go with the discussion flow and be flexible when exchanging ideas.

You are now ready for the last stage of learning with cases, the large group or class discussion. Set yourself up for some excitement and illumination. Relax. Enjoy.

large group discussion

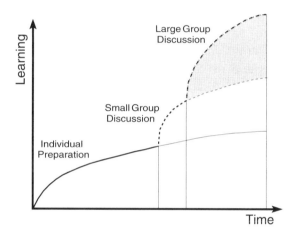

The third stage of the case learning process consists of the large group or class discussion. The collective efforts of all class participants aided by an instructor provide a further chance to lift your learning level higher. Achieving group synergy requires commitment from the whole group to make the best possible use of the time available and to search together for superior insights. The comparison to a live orchestra performance is a good analogy. Practice time is over. Each member now has to play his or her instrument to assure a quality performance. However, different from orchestras who play to a set of musical scores, case discussion allows considerable individual freedom to influence the outcome.

This chapter will clarify the large group discussion process. Meaningful class contribution is the central theme. Effective participation suggestions will be provided throughout.

THE LARGE GROUP OR CLASS DISCUSSION PROCESS

A standard large group discussion process does not exist. Case classes often appear to be disorderly and lacking in substance to a casual observer. "Good discussions unfold in unexpected ways that modify the programmed logic of a teaching plan," says Christensen from the Harvard Business School (*Education for Judgment* 106). Discussion process variations depend on the class objectives, the subject matter, the type of case, the place in the sequence of classes, previous classes, or other classes in other courses taken simultaneously by the same students. Additional sources of variation include the teaching style of the instructor, the chemistry of the class, the mood of the participants, the time of the year and the physical facility.

Even though a standard case class does not exist, many case classes possess the following chronological phases: (1) In-class-pre-class; (2) Pre-case or "warm-up"; (3) Case discussion; (4) Post-case or closing.

1. In-Class - Pre-Class

The in-class-pre-class phase relates to what happens in the classroom, including the interactions between the arriving students and the instructor, before class starts. During this phase there is an opportunity to organize and glance at your notes; get into the mood of the case; check briefly a point of analysis with a classmate; cheer up an uneasy colleague; or tell the instructor that you wish to volunteer to start the discussion. Many instructors welcome this initiative. Occasionally, to save class time, an instructor may ask, "Does anyone have an answer to this assignment that we can put on the board or show on the screen?" Take the opportunity to have your work recognized.

2. Pre-Case or "Warm-up"

In many case classes, the discussion of the case is not the first item on the agenda. Different types of activities set the stage for the discussion or "warm-up" the class:

a) *Greetings, announcements, general comments, or a humorous story* get class attention and silence.

b) *Review of previous classes* helps reinforce points or tidy up loose ends. Be ready to contribute extra insights if there is a chance. Ask for clarification if something is still not clear.

c) *Assignments for future cases* provide helpful advice.

d) *News items* brought in by the instructor or you are useful to relate case issues to current events.

e) *Discussion of readings and theoretical concepts* is used to check understanding. Take the opportunity to comment on or ask a question about a concept you or your small group wrestled with. Be prepared to respond to questions from the instructor as well.

f) *Course context discussion explains how the case fits within the course.* Instructors may review the last few classes to show the sequence leading to this particular case, or stress the importance of the case to the course.

g) *Anecdotes and experience* from instructors or class members may serve as an introduction to the case.

All or none of these pre-case activities may happen. Some instructors will jump right into the case discussion and skip any of the preliminaries.

3. The Case Discussion

The "normal" case discussion will cover at least five phases:
(1) the start; (2) the issue(s) identification; (3) the analysis; (4) the
alternatives and decision; and (5) the action and implementation
plan. These phases parallel the case solving model
recommended for individual preparation (see Chapter 3).

1. Start

Some instructors start the class discussion by asking
someone (or several participants) for his or her solution to the
case and then work backwards to derive the analysis. Other
instructors start by asking for a definition of the issue(s) at
stake and proceed in a logical manner towards the solution
and implementation.

The opening question may be specific or broad and open-
ended, depending on the style of the facilitator. A directive
instructor may ask, "If you were Ms. Jones, would you accept
the terms of agreement as presented by Mr. Clark and why?"
A non-directive teacher may simply say, "How would you like
to start the class?" You may be given a few minutes notice to
collect your thoughts or you may have to answer immediately.

Some instructors come to class with a plan to call on one or
more participants at the beginning of (or throughout) the class.
Other instructors may expect individual class members to
volunteer when they believe they can make a meaningful
contribution to the discussion.

If you are called upon or wish to volunteer to start the class
take advantage of this opportunity to say anything you believe
to be meaningful. Because the slate is clean, you do not need to
worry about previous comments from your classmates.
However, your comments will provide the basis for further
discussion. Therefore, it is useful to take your time and to
explain your insights logically and clearly so that others can
connect their subsequent observations in a meaningful

manner. Many instructors use a simple rule, "As long as the person who starts the class is making sense, I'll let him or her continue." So, do not feel you are being rushed — take the time necessary to explain your insights from the first two stages of the case learning process.

Effective starting contributions to a case class discussion include:

"If I were in this person's position in this case, I would concentrate on this issue because it is both strategic and urgent..."

"As sales manager in this case, I would recognize that there are a number of factors that led to this situation, such as..."

"My analysis of this case suggests that the best decision is to... and it is really critical that the first three action steps... be completed by the end of next week."

"First I would like to address the key issue, then the alternatives and, finally, my recommendations..."

2. *The Issue(s) Identification*

Normally, at some stage of the class discussion (although not necessarily at the beginning), considerable deliberation takes place to identify the exact nature of the issue(s) in the case. In some cases this task is trivial because the answer is obvious; in other cases it may constitute the central educational challenge of the discussion.

Useful contributions for clarifying the issues include:

"Going into my small group I believed the key issue was..., but Jane persuaded me that... should be the major issue because..."

"I believe this is the key decision we need to focus on because..."

"I think the issue is broader than stated by Robert, because..."

"There are three decisions that need to be taken and this is the sequence in which they should be taken..."

"I say this because the following three items... are all symptoms of a larger issue which is ..."

"The immediate issue is ... and the basic issues are ..."

3.   *Case Data Analysis*

With a focus on the above issue(s), case class discussions turn to an analysis of the evidence or causal sequence of events. This stage of the discussion is where the tools, techniques, concepts and theories are used to help make sense of both quantitative and qualitative information available.

Typical analytical contributions are:

"The symptom in this case is..., but the causes are..."

"My calculations show that..."

"If Paula's calculations are correct, then the implications are..."

"Because of the following constraints... it will be difficult to..."

"If we use the concept of ..., which I think fits perfectly with the problem we are considering because ..., then the conclusion that falls out is..."

"My consumer analysis says that potential customers will first consider price and then..."

"The relevant information is contained in the exhibit on page seven."

4. Alternatives and Decision

A significant part of most case classes deals with the discussion of alternatives. You will be asked to generate them, discuss their respective merits in depth, identify your decision criteria, present your arguments and justify your decision(s) or recommendation(s).

Effective contributions for the alternatives and decision phase include:

"There are at least three alternatives which appear to have merits and they are: ..."

"Even though the financial return on this alternative is so exceptional, I think we need to make absolutely sure that the environmental concerns are effectively addressed. "

"Since qualitatively and quantitatively this alternative is so attractive, it makes the decision to go with this alternative very easy."

"Since this alternative would take at least three years to implement, it is just not realistic given our short term crisis."

"The risk inherent in Bill's proposal is ... because ..."

"Another alternative I would like to propose is ... for the following reasons ..."

"The decision is very close. On the one hand ... whereas on the other hand ... Given these I slightly favor ... because ..."

Class consensus about the best alternative or decision may not emerge, as it may well be that more than one alternative is fully reasonable, even after careful examination.

5. Action and Implementation Plan

Discussion of action and implementation strategies and tactics sometimes receives scant attention in case classes because some instructors believe proper identification and analysis of the problem and discussion of theory are more important. Also, since implementation is logically discussed at the end of class, it often gets lost in the race with the clock. How decisions are executed can be as significant as what decisions are made to solve a problem or address an issue.

Examples of action and implementation plan contributions are:

"To install this new equipment in the same physical location as the old one, we will need to build up inventory of at least one month to assure continuing flow of product to the customer."

"The first thing we'd have to do, if we follow Kim's proposed solution, is to get approval from the Board, which would take at least three months, then ..."

"To meet the deadline of January 15, at least twenty people will have to work on this over the next six months and the following three departments are going to have to provide them ..."

"First I will have to go out and gather the information that is still missing. If it comes out as ... then I will have to do this...; if not, I would take the following steps..."

"I would pay careful attention to ... in the future."

4. Post-Case or Closing

The class conclusion is a transition phase. It can be used to close the current discussion, link it to subsequent classes or to the ones so far completed. A student may be asked to summarize the case and its key points, although many instructors do it themselves. Sometimes instructors' summaries will take the form of questions left for students to ponder after class. Other times, the instructor will summarize and provide his or her own framework and analytical insights that may cover some of the key points discussed in class and attempt to pull the discussion all together.

If the instructor asks you to summarize or you choose to volunteer to "pull the case together," this is a good opportunity to synthesize. For example, "Having come into class with only two alternatives, I was surprised to find that there were three more just as feasible... What we learned from the theory... we covered in the last two classes really helped in putting this decision into perspective with respect to...," or "Seeing where we managed to end this class compared to the way I came in, I can really see the benefits of ..."

With little time remaining to the end of the class, you can contribute by saying, "Because we are running out of time, I will skip past some less relevant points and go directly to the main conclusion and implementation..." It is a useful reminder that everyone in class, not just the instructor, should be sensitive to time.

If the case has been very well discussed, several options for further contributions exist. One may be to move to a basic issue discussion: "In this example, the choice of the latest and best technology appeared relatively easy. Surely, there are other situations where this decision might not be so clear cut. For example..." Another could be to enhance an earlier contribution: "I believe that in this case discussion the comments from Helen really moved us a long way into the right direction. Once we could see how the information in Exhibit 1 could be combined with Exhibit 4, the analysis and need for action became crystal clear."

The Instructor's Solution and What Really Happened

Regardless of how the discussion closes, students should not expect the instructor to provide his or her solution. Most instructors resist offering students a personal solution so as not to demotivate them from continuing to search for their own answers.

It is also unlikely that instructors will reveal what the organization actually did. For one thing, they may not know what happened. Even if they know, they are obligated not to violate confidences and disguises. In any event, most of the time, it really does not matter what management actually did. What is relevant is how you and your classmates dealt with this case based on the information given. Some instructors believe that disclosure of the actual decision taken tends to provide premature closure to the case. Your mind will keep working away on unresolved issues much longer than on situations where the instructor told you what actually happened in the organization.

STAKEHOLDERS IN THE
CLASSROOM DISCUSSION PROCESS

Christensen expresses a fundamental insight at the core of the discussion process: "...teaching and learning are inseparable, parts of a single continuum ... of reciprocal giving and receiving. In discussion pedagogy students share the teaching task with the instructor and one another. All teach, and all learn" (*Education for Judgment* 99). While students and instructors share the learning and teaching tasks, their respective roles have nevertheless a distinct focus.

The Instructor

The key focus of the instructor's role is to facilitate the discussion and to provide opportunity for students to maximize their learning. Christensen conveys the challenge associated with this role: "What is a discussion, if not a voyage of exploration, with the leader as both captain and crew member?" (*Education for Judgment* 106). Some instructors tend to be more directive or of the "captain" type; others more non-directive or of the "crew" type. There is no one best way of teaching. Instructors complement each other and at times will embrace different approaches. It would be very boring if all instructors behaved exactly the same way in the classroom.

Normally, instructors evaluate and record class contributions shortly after class. When you are taking a course which uses a reasonable number of cases, you should know whether class contribution counts toward your final grade and for how much of the grade. All the comments in this book about effective learning with cases apply whether your class contribution is graded or not. However, if class participation is graded and you do not participate in the large group discussion at all, you are not only losing a valuable opportunity to learn more, but you may also put your course grade at risk.

The Participants

Your role in the case class discussion is to learn through listening, talking and reflecting. As for your responsibilities, these are well summarized by Shapiro of the Harvard Business School as he encourages students to be committed to the "4Ps" of involvement in case discussion: "preparation, presence, promptness and participation" ("Hints for Case Teaching"). In other words, your responsibilities are to do your homework, to attend class, to be on time and to partake in the discussion. This is the minimum. To maximize learning, however, your participation must truly contribute to the discussion. You have to be willing to share your analysis, to subject your ideas to open debate, to take risks, and to critique others' positions in a positive manner.

PARTICIPATION IN THE LARGE GROUP DISCUSSION

In the large group discussion learning depends upon each student's giving to, as well as taking from, each session.

Without full and regular participation, development of knowledge and skills will be compromised. Easton from the Management School of the University of Lancaster summarizes it well: "Case discussions provide an excellent example of the old adage, 'You only get out what you put in.' It is not difficult to 'hide' throughout a course which relies on discussion in a large student group, but the educational opportunity cost is very great. You can learn a great deal and develop skills quickly in the hothouse atmosphere of case discussion. It would be a pity to throw that chance away" (190). Seeing participation not as a problem, but as an opportunity with high pay-off, allows you to develop a repertoire of skills directly connected to success and effectiveness in your chosen profession.

Effective Participation

Effective participation involves not only speaking, but also active listening and reflecting. Meaningful contributions relate to case content as well as the discussion process. Both types are valuable although content contributions occupy most of the class time.

Content contributions derive mostly from your individual and small group preparation based on the information contained in the case along with your collateral experience. Content contributions separate facts from opinions; provide a significant chunk of analysis, an alternative not previously identified, critical quantitative analysis, identification of reasonable assumptions, or an action or implementation plan. In essence, this kind of contribution adds breadth, depth and understanding to the discussion of the case. The previous section, describing the various chronological phases of a case class, contains good examples of content contributions.

Process contributions affect the flow and structure of the discussion. They are based on good listening and reflecting skills, as well as your understanding of the case. Process contributions include: questions that add clarity; suggestions that a certain area of the case needs to be explored; a linkage of points raised earlier; a call to order if the discussion has gone off topic; or a meaningful summary. Exhibit 5-1 provides examples of a variety of process contributions.

Exhibit 5-1
EXAMPLES OF USEFUL PROCESS CONTRIBUTIONS

I think...

1. we should start by..., move to...
2. we should next talk about...
3. we need to spend more (or less) time on...
4. we should go back to Jack's point...
5. we need some more explanations of...
6. we need more clarification on how theory applies here
7. we should get back on topic
8. we need to resolve this difference of opinion before we can move on
9. we should hear from Jane because...

Raising Your Hand

In most case discussions it is normal for participants who wish to speak to put up their hand. Usually, the instructor indicates that a particular individual can speak next, or may even indicate a sequence: "Susan first, then John, then Mary." There are times when the discussion will bypass this formal routine and class members jump into the discussion without the instructor's intervention. Be prepared for either mode. You control whether your hand goes up, not whether the instructor will ask you to speak. Frequency, although important, is not as important as quality. Therefore, you should be ready to contribute in every class and throughout the course you should receive your fair share of opportunities to speak.

The Right and the Wrong Answer

Effective participation does not mean you have to have an answer to every question and to be right all the time. It is acceptable to admit you don't know at times. Nevertheless, you are encouraged to experiment and take risks; there is certainly no punishment for giving the wrong answer. On the contrary, as Christensen explains, "In the discussion process, "wrong" can be more helpful than "right"; an obtuse statement can spark a charged, enlightening debate that straightforward analysis could never provide" (*Education for Judgment* 106).

Quality Versus Quantity

In any given class, not everyone can participate, especially when class size exceeds 30 students. In an 80 minute class, for example, it is difficult to have more than 25 to 30 people participate in the discussion in a meaningful way. Often, students do not participate but have lots of "gold nuggets" to offer. The correlation between willingness and ability to participate is not always positive. Sometimes, students participate but their comments are weak and shallow. It is not how much you say that counts but the relevance of what you say to solving the case or adding to the wisdom of the class. When you get the floor, take the time necessary to make your point(s) clearly. Some students seem to think they are only allowed ten seconds.

The question as to how long to talk when you have the floor is not easy. Typically, at the start of the class longer discourses are normal. When the filling-in process starts, class contributions may be shorter. For example, "Another advantage of this alternative is the relatively low cost of implementation." Most contributions in case discussions tend to be too short rather than too long. Participants say, "I prefer alternative B" and leave out the "because..." Then the instructor has to start "pulling teeth" by asking "why" and saying "please expand on your point" over and over again.

Ineffective Participation

To clarify effective participation further, it is useful to devote some time to its opposite. Ineffective participation involves comments that do not build or add value to the content or process of the discussion.

Simply repeating case facts, as opposed to using them to re-emphasize or build on an analysis, is a very common type of ineffective participation. For example, "This company is located in the western part of the country; it has about 5,000 employees and has been in existence since 1982" is not a class contribution. It just repeats case facts. This is quite different from: "Because the company is located in the western part of the country and the primary market is in the eastern part, the logistics of getting its products to market represent a significant challenge;" or "Because the company has 5,000 employees it is not realistic that the new president can establish a personal relationship with each of them." These last two contributions properly link case facts to analytical insights.

Repeating someone else's comments just because a participant wants to be heard or was not listening wastes class time.

Inconsequential interjections of the "I agree" type, without explaining why, do not add value to the discussion.

Unrealistic assumptions can be a convenient substitute for rigorous case analysis (see Chapter 3 on individual preparation for more information about assumptions). An extreme example of such shallow intervention would be, "I'm assuming that the union will not agree with proposals one and two and therefore I will propose my own solution to this situation which I'm assuming they will accept."

Using questions to deflect the discussion is counter-productive. Asking the instructor for his or her opinion or experience on a certain topic may be seen as a delaying tactic to keep the instructor talking instead of addressing the issue(s). Similarly, asking for more information about the case or for the instructor's solution will not be valued.

Digressions in the form of irrelevant, off-topic or out-of-place comments are dysfunctional. Examples include references to some personal anecdote or past experience having little or no relevance to the case situation. Some of these comments stem from a need for some students to show off in front of their colleagues. Most digressions, however, are not conscious ones; they come from inexperience with case discussion and inability to listen and build on what has been said by other members of the class.

Monopolizing the discussion involves taking too much of the class time and, therefore, excluding others. Verbose students tend to get on the nerves of the class and frequently the class itself will use social pressure to cool them off over time.

Being disengaged is illustrated by students who show little interest in the class discussion by surfing the Web, reading a newspaper, looking bored, sleeping, or looking away from the person who is taking. They rarely contribute anything. When they engage in the discussion, their comments are shallow, off-topic, or unfocused. Their input consists mostly of short contributions that add little to the discussion.

Being uncivil with comments that attack, ridicule or put down colleagues will anger some, silence others, and certainly damage the overall discussion and underlying chemistry of the class. Students will be defensive, resist modifying their positions, or refrain from participating. Confrontation rather than exploration will become the name of the game. To turn a group of students into a learning community, Christensen endorses civility as the first basic value for this purpose. "In class as elsewhere, politeness sets a cooperative tone and encourages the openness that lets people help one another by sharing experience and insight" (*Education for Judgment* 20).

PERSONAL STRATEGIES AND TACTICS
FOR MANAGING YOUR CONTRIBUTIONS

The secret to effective participation in a case discussion is to listen and think at the same time. Most people only talk about one fifth as fast as they think, therefore students have ample opportunity to review, reflect and organize their thoughts while others are talking. Of course many other factors will affect your participation.

Instructor Related Factors. The teaching style and skills of the instructor will have an impact on your participation. Is the instructor directive or not? Is he or she using the 'carrot' or the 'nail' approach? That is, is the approach gently to invite students' participation or to force it on them? Some instructors will ask for volunteers; some will notify in advance the students they will call upon; others will ask students randomly or use a pre-determined call list. And finally, does the instructor have specific expectations? For example, he or she may reject "one-liner" comments and insist that students speak in paragraphs to lay out their thoughts. If such expectations exist, try to meet them.

Student Related Factors. Your own personality, background, experience and culture will affect your participation. Some people are by nature more outspoken than others and will enter the discussion spontaneously without even waiting to be called upon. We all have our own strengths and weaknesses. Draw on your personal strengths and special abilities in contributing to class, recognizing that these will evolve over time.

Materials Related Factors. Course content and the cases themselves will influence your willingness and ability to participate. Is the subject matter of the course related to your past studies or some special expertise? Is the case set in a familiar industry? It is always easier to talk about something you are familiar with and you may bring a unique perspective to the discussion.

The answers to all these questions will affect your contribution to class. Next, follow some suggestions that have not been made earlier about your input in class, effective listening, note-taking, and dealing with specific challenges to participation.

Inputs to Class

Use your preparation notes. To guide your input as well as to keep track of the various points being made, refer to the notes you developed in your individual and small group preparation. The Case Preparation Chart (Exhibit 3-2) can easily be used for this purpose. You may wish to tick off the various ideas and thoughts your notes contain as points are made by you and your colleagues in the evolving discussion. This will help your concentration, prevent duplication of contribution, and remind you of complementary or additional points you may wish to make.

Organize your remarks. It is good practice to relate your contribution to what has been said before: "Joe has already given two reasons why this alternative would be attractive, I would like to add two more..." Using a simple structure, such as a list, can also be useful to keep track of your thoughts. State your ideas one point at a time and be clear and concise.

Time Your Remarks. It is wise to wait for the right time to introduce your ideas. Easton recommends practice in the process of subjugating your own needs to those of the group. "Don't throw in the brilliant, but irrelevant, idea you have just had. Wait until the time is ripe and it becomes a relevant issue" (190).

Consider various discussion roles. You can contribute in a variety of roles in class and may wish to experiment with content and process roles. The following list describes four content roles:

1. the "Expert" who has profound knowledge of the industry, one or more of the issues, or some other specific aspect of the case;
2. the "Veteran" who brings his or her personal experience to the case discussion;
3. the "Social Conscience" who introduces ethical considerations or social issues into the discussion;
4. the "Galvanizer" who offers key or unique insights that galvanize attention or truly inspire everyone.

Other roles are related to the discussion process. For example:

5. the "Rescuer" who saves the discussion when it reaches an impasse;
6. the "Impersonator" who vividly takes on the role of one of the case characters, not necessarily the key one;
7. the "Interrogator" who questions other students in a way that challenges and pushes forward their analysis;
8. the "Traffic Cop" who gets the discussion back on track;
9. the "Devil's Advocate" who provokes the class to look at the other side of the coin;
10. the "Mediator" who offers compromise between two extreme positions; and
11. the "Referee" who settles arguments.

Effective Listening

Many students have problems with listening; they just wait for their turn to speak or are too busy thinking about what they are going to say. Poor listening creates repetition and discussions that go in circles and lead nowhere. For the discussion process to improve over time, it is important that you develop the art and skills of active listening. This will impact not only on the relevance of your contributions but also on their timing and on your overall learning from others.

One aspect of active listening is concentrating not only on what is being said but what it means. Listening is said to take as much effort as speaking. Professor Learned stresses the need to listen with an open mind: "One's preconceptions and experiences limit, so much, the capacity to hear and understand. It often takes a long time to really hear and understand another's spoken or implied words and feelings" (Christensen & Hansen, *Teaching and the Case Method* 10). The focus is therefore on listening for the total meaning, which includes the verbal and non-verbal parts of the message, or the content plus the underlying attitudes and values that are conveyed.

In case discussion, active listening includes an evaluative component. You have to compare what is said with your own ideas and positions. Do you agree with what is said? Why? Why not? Answers to these questions will certainly help you participate in the discussion.

Note-Taking

To focus your attention, assist your active listening and help you retain the information for later review, it is useful to take some notes during class. These notes may take the form of simple annotations, possibly using a different color pen, on your existing preparation notes. They may consist of ideas, insights, concepts, principles, reminders, generalizations or discoveries that will add to your preparation notes. In order for these notes to help and not hamper your participation, they must be brief, to the point, and selective. Some students use note-taking as a way of hiding from the instructor. They think that by feverishly writing everything down the instructor will see this behavior as a form of attentiveness and leave them alone. There is no need to record in detail what happens in class. Notes should act as memory triggers when you reflect and summarize your thoughts after class.

Dealing with Specific Challenges to Participation

If you find it difficult to speak up in class. The most common problem in class discussion is that a significant number of participants are shy or afraid to participate. The longer you wait, the more difficult it will be to speak up. To help you get started, here are some proven suggestions:

1. Good preparation is the key. Use Chapters 3 and 4 to make sure you are well prepared and confident.

2. Adopt an offensive attitude, psych yourself to participate in class. Do not wait for the instructor to call on you. This way you have more control over your contributions.

3. Ask the instructor ahead of time if you can start the class and, if it is accepted, prepare for it. Look for a case that you like and feel comfortable with. Of course, starting off the class once is not a substitute for regular preparation and participation; it is only to help you break the ice.

4. Try making eye contact and speaking to a few people you know will support you, such as members of your small group, and try blocking off the rest of the class.

5. Psychologically reduce the size of the class by choosing a seat close to the front.

6. Make a deal with one of your classmates who appears to face the same challenge to see who can participate most often in a week. Keep a record of your respective contributions. Make it a little contest with an appropriate incentive for the winner such as a free lunch, a drink, a movie or a dollar.

7. Force yourself to raise your hand at least once in each class.

8. If you feel a serious blockage, do not hesitate to speak to your instructor. He or she will make it easier for you to participate in the discussion, either by giving you pointers

or by simply being more attentive to the subtle signals you give when you are ready to speak.

Some programs have a system of an advisor, mentor, or buddy for each student. It is wise to take advantage of such resources at any time and especially if the fear of participation escalates. For a number of students, it can become a vicious circle. They become concerned about their low participation, try to do something about it, fail, feel bad about failing, try again, fail again, and feel worse yet. That negative spiral needs to be broken or it can lead to some serious problems.

In our experience, once you acknowledge that you have a problem and are willing to deal with it, it is often half solved already. Your instructor, advisor, mentor or counselor will probably start by exploring with you where the problem lies, what is the cause of your low participation. Does it occur in every course or only in one? Are you a quiet person? Are you discouraged? Do you feel insecure? Are you participating in your small group discussion? Is the fear of talking in class based on a lack of adequate preparation or on a feeling of inferiority? Once agreement has been reached on the causes, you can start planning remedial action, setting reasonable participation goals and a monitoring or support system. Taking little steps, one at a time, and reporting to your advisor on a regular basis are effective ways of dealing with this all too common challenge.

If you are not certain of your case analysis. At times you may feel that you have not "cracked" the case. Despite your best efforts in individual and small group preparation, you still are not comfortable with the results. Thus, if the instructor asks you to participate you are somewhat reluctant. Exhibit 5-2 gives suggestions as to how to deal with such a situation effectively, what to avoid and why.

Exhibit 5-2
CONTRIBUTING WHEN NOT CERTAIN
(Including Potential Reactions from Classmates or the Instructor)

Effective Comments	Ineffective Comments
"I don't think I have a complete handle on this case, but this is as far as I got." (Your classmates and instructors know you tried to do your best.)	"This case does not make any sense to me." (Did you even read it?)
"This is the kind of calculation I would have done if I had had more time. This is why I think this calculation is important because it would have provided an answer to this question and, if this answer were positive, I would do the following... and if the answer were negative, this is what I would do differently..." (It shows you have been thinking and in what direction.)	"I did not want to calculate anything because the numbers looked strange;" or "I did not have a calculator;" or "I was not sure what the numbers meant." (It shows you have really not pushed this very hard.)
"I did not get as far as implementation because I did not think it useful to worry about implementation until I had the right alternative figured out and I think that implementation of any of the alternatives under consideration will not likely affect this decision." (You've been thinking.)	"Implementation? Well, implementation is clearly important. Maybe we should worry about a short and a long term plan. Yeah, implementation." (Are you trying to bluff your way through?)
"I don't know." (Honesty pays.)	"I think I know but if we go back to that earlier alternative we discarded, I think I can find another reason for discarding it." (Well, if it's dead, let it lie.)

If you are not prepared or will not attend. If you know you are going to be away, it is good practice to let the instructor know beforehand and, if possible, to provide a hand-in for the class. Your copy of the Case Preparation Chart (Exhibit 3-2) is an impressive reminder to the instructor that you are taking the course seriously despite your absence.

Occasionally circumstances may make it impossible for you to be prepared for a case discussion class. If this happens, tell your instructor before the class starts that you are not prepared to participate in the discussion. Waiting to see if you will be asked in class is seen as "playing games," hoping that you will not be discovered. It is not a good idea to come regularly unprepared to class.

If the language spoken by the class is a second language to you. Be aware that you may be slower to react than your classmates. The timing of your interventions may not be right. Normally, your ability to understand the second language will precede ability to speak it. Starting the discussion may be easier for you as you will have more control over your contribution and less chance to repeat someone else's comments. Your instructor should be made aware of your specific challenge. But do not use it as an excuse for not getting involved. You will be surprised how tolerant the class will be of your mistakes. And you will learn more by speaking.

If you are asked to play a certain role or to improvise. The key to effective role playing during case discussion is to identify with the actor in the case. You now have to take on the age, gender, and personality of the person whose role you are playing. This task is quite different from your normal case analysis role of putting yourself into the position, but not the skin, of the decision maker. Try to be realistic in this assignment.

If you represent a minority within the class, because of your race, your culture, your gender, your sexual orientation or your background, be aware that you may be more conspicuous. It will be harder to hide in the group and at the same time, particularly if you are of the shy type, you may feel self-conscious and find it difficult to participate. You could even become a victim of discriminatory remarks. Do not hesitate to denounce such comments and, if needed, press for your rights.

If your culture is based on values different from the prevailing ones of the class, making an honest attempt to identify what these value differences are will help you to understand why people talk and act the way they do. Understanding is the key to communication.

Be aware that the diversity you bring to the class is positive and enriching. Learning to work with people who are different is extremely valuable.

AFTER CLASS REFLECTION

As it is difficult to participate and observe or evaluate at the same time, it is essential that you take a few moments to reflect on your learning experience after each class. With so much emphasis on learning by doing, this is especially important with the case discussion. While regular class contributions will certainly help you hone the various skills that can be developed with the case method, you must be aware that repetition can also reinforce bad habits. Therefore it is imperative that your class contributions be subject to on-going self-evaluation to seek improvement in future classes.

This after class reflection is also required to improve future learning and to sharpen your skills in all three stages of learning: individual preparation, small group and large group discussions. It will also help you prepare for case exams.

Take no more than five minutes as soon as possible after class, while your memory is fresh, to record and summarize your key observations, insights or generalizations. Do not put off this task past the same day or the learning may well vanish from your conscious mind, as you move to the next case learning cycle. After all the time that you have already put on the case, these few extra minutes have a high pay-off.

After class reflection allows you to complete your Case Preparation Chart. This reflective task encompasses more than the classroom discussion. Your reflection and evaluative comments may relate to (1) the case content; (2) yourself; and (3) the group and participation of others. Here are some questions under each category which may help you engage in this evaluative process.

1. *Case Content Evaluation.* Did you understand what this case was all about? (If you did not, you should get help from your classmates or instructor.) What lessons did you learn from this case?

2. *Self-Evaluation.* Given your individual preparation, what did you add to the small group and to the large group discussion? What did you learn in terms of your own ability to make decisions? Did you make the same mistakes as before? What can you do to avoid repetitive mistakes? How could you have handled this preparation and participation better? What did you learn about yourself for the future?

3. *Group Evaluation.* What did you learn in terms of where the class is in the course? What is it about the case that the class missed? What did your small group add or contribute to the large discussion?

ETHICAL CONSIDERATIONS

In closing this chapter, some important ethical considerations need to be stressed.

1. All of your class notes are personal. You should not share them with anyone other than your own class members.

Making notes available to others for free or for a fee is not a good idea.

2. You should abstain from discussing a case with students from other classes who will have it later.

3. Never attempt to obtain the instructor's teaching guide, manual or personal notes.

4. Do not contact the organization about which the case is written to find out what decision was taken or what happened subsequently.

These admonitions are all based on the premise that case learning cannot be borrowed. It has to be developed and owned outright by each student. Case learning is similar to mountain climbing. It may be possible to reach the mountain top via helicopter, but flying there is not the same as climbing there. According to Frederick, "The key to effective retention of learning, I believe, is in owning the discovery" (Christensen & Hansen, *Teaching and the Case Method* 216). If you bypass the above rules, not only will you greatly diminish the learning experience of other students but you may also force the instructor to discard good material. Case development is expensive; the value and the inventory of cases will suffer greatly if documented learning about such cases leaks out.

Every class member has a responsibility to assist in creating a positive learning atmosphere in the case discussion session. You can help those who are struggling with the material and/or the process by being supportive and patient. The creation of a caring class atmosphere as well as one dedicated to high standards of accomplishment is a serious ethical challenge imposed by the case method.

case presentations, reports and exams

Cases are sometimes used in ways other than the typical classroom discussion. Three traditional variants are case presentations, case reports and case exams. Instructors will have their own reasons for using cases in these three forms as well as personal preferences regarding their execution.

The one common element for all three variants is that they require a thorough individual preparation as described in Chapter 3. We will not provide much detail on effective writing or the making of presentations since specialized communication texts are readily available.

CASE PRESENTATIONS

Types of presentation

Presentations of a case in class vary. Some instructors will ask the small groups in their pre-class discussion to select a spokesperson to present the group viewpoint to the class. This format supposes that each group will have reached a consensus on the case. Some instructors use this format routinely in lieu of large group discussion because it forces students to prepare. However, it can be rather stifling, leading to various groups repeating the same points, missing learning opportunities, especially for the non-presenting students.

To offset this last weakness, some instructors assign roles to the non-presenters or limit the number of presentations to only one or two groups per class. For example, one structured approach to presentation might involve the selection of two analyst groups to present the case and two critic groups to appraise the presentations, and raise questions or counter-arguments, while the remaining class members assume the role of directors or stockholders of the firm.

To involve non-presenting students or observers, some instructors use a brief evaluation sheet that each member of the class fills out for each presentation and hands to the presenting teams at the end of the class. Other instructors will ask the non-presenters to submit their position paper on the case the next day. This paper, less detailed than the group presentation, is a response to the presenters' position(s).

Sometimes the presentation is done on an individual basis and resembles the real world briefing of senior management by a junior executive or the presentation made by a consultant to the staff of an organization.

Some cases lend themselves to staging a debate, with the teams either chosen in advance or formed at the start of the class. This approach may involve a role play or a town hall meeting format. It works well with cases where a choice must be made between at least two alternative courses of action, where each alternative has both strong positive and negative aspects and no single alternative is clearly preferable.

Other variations on the theme include formal case competitions, with different groups within a school or between schools presenting the case in front of a jury; the presence in class of executive visitors; and the taping of the presentations followed by debriefing sessions.

Suggestions for Effective Presentations

Whatever the type of presentation, there are some common elements and requirements to take into account. Sound individual preparation and small group discussion are still prerequisites. Next, the focus shifts to execution: how to communicate your group's ideas effectively. The manner in which you express these ideas will have significant impact on their acceptance. Here are some practical suggestions:

Organize your presentation. In group presentations, considerable thought must be placed on who says what and in which order. Special care should be devoted to your opening to arouse interest and get the class attention; and to your conclusion as it may provide a lasting impression.

Make sure you have a clear structure. Referring occasionally to this structure will also help your audience retain the important information. "If the skeleton does not hang together, the flesh can never be put on the bones," says Easton (194).

Prepare well. A good preparation is the key to an effective presentation. It builds self-confidence. It does not mean, however, a full write-up of what you are going to say and then reading it. This is often boring and makes direct contact with the audience difficult. Easton notes, "Oral presentations are in many ways easier to plan for than classroom discussion. The structure of the discussion is under your control since you, or a member of your group, will be the only one speaking" (191).

Use memory props. An outline of your key points rather than the exact words, cue cards, succinct overhead transparencies or computer generated graphics will serve as a guide to your presentation while preserving your ability to react to the audience and allowing for some spontaneity.

Keep it simple. A common flaw of many presentations is to pack in too much information. Only the key points will be remembered anyway. So keep your structure or outline simple.

Use quality visual aids.   Illustrating your presentation with quality and pertinent visual aids will certainly enhance your presentation. These aids should be simple and complement, not detract from your presentation. Effective use of slides, transparencies or computer graphics may actually save time, as it allows you to cut down on lengthy descriptions and explanations.

Computerized projection offers a wide range of color, motion, sound and graphics options. One word of warning, however. This technology, while allowing for creativity, should not dominate your performance. It should remain what it is, an aid. Do not let the glitz overpower the message. Avoid filling in the screen with too much detail. If you are using computer graphics, be sure the technology works and is set up before you begin, to avoid any delay during the presentation.

Rehearse.   Make sure that your rehearsal is not just for content but also for style of delivery, eye contact, poise, timing, linking between various presenters and use of visual aids. Beware of mannerisms and do not hesitate to ask for feedback. Rehearsal will also help build your confidence.

Anticipate your audience reaction.   If you spend some time trying to anticipate the questions from the audience, you will be in a better position to defend your positions.

Suggestions for Critic-Observers

Be constructive. If you have to give feedback, make sure your comments are descriptive, clear, honest and objective; for example, "This is what I saw you do:..." as opposed to "I did not like your..." Only then will they be helpful to the presenter. If you comment on weaknesses, be tactful. It is best to present the good points first.

Limit your observations to a few important aspects of the presentation.   You will be a more effective observer if you focus on some key aspects of the presentation, especially if you are new to this role, rather than try to report on everything. With experience, you may add other aspects to your remarks.

Distinguish between content and process observations. Content observations relate to factors such as the logic of arguments, pertinence of recommendations, soundness of assumptions or clarity of ideas. Process observations deal with the structure of the presentation, effective use of visual aids and the ability to connect with the audience.

Learn vicariously. Your role as critic or observer can be a tremendous learning experience. Hopefully, observation of and feedback from others will help you improve your own presentations.

CASE REPORTS

Types of Report

Sometimes case reports are used in conjunction with case discussion or even presentation. In the first instance, they may be handed in before or after class and are often used to test the quality of student preparation. They may consist of no more than case preparation notes. In the second instance, they may be required by the instructor to accompany a presentation for evaluation purposes. They may consist of a compilation of the presentation transparencies and handouts.

This section focuses on a more formal type of written case report that is polished and stands alone, although it may represent an individual or a group effort. The distinguishing features of this type of report, as opposed to case class discussion or an exam, are the rigorous analysis and attention to presentation. As some people say, "Reports are power tests. Exams are speed tests." The challenge of case reports is to convey effectively your complete analysis and specific recommendations in written form.

The case report presupposes the same type of individual preparation as for case discussion (see Chapter 3) but a more exhaustive one. It may allow for small group discussion (see Chapter 4), whether a group or individual report is required. In the latter case, many instructors permit common exhibits which credit the appropriate contributors while the report must represent an individual effort.

Suggestions for Effective Case Reports

The following suggestions may be helpful for effective case report preparation.

Check the assignment. Start by considering who will receive this report, what its purpose is and whether there are any special requirements. For example, the case assignment often requires you to assume a position. "In your position as marketing manager of Zing Corporation, write a report on your recommendations to the president," is a common type of assignment. In this example, the needs of the president should direct your efforts. Make sure you also meet other requirements, such as those pertaining to length, style, and format.

Review the evaluation criteria. Typically, written reports are evaluated according to the following criteria: clear identification of the issue(s); soundness and accuracy of analysis; legitimacy, range and evaluation of alternatives; appropriateness and specificity of recommendations, including action and implementation plans; consistency of logic; and the quality of the written presentation.

Plan your report carefully. Experience has clearly proven the usefulness of planning your approach to the report carefully. Determining in advance what to put where and how much to include has major pay-offs. Such planning will not only facilitate the writing of the report but also result in better grades.

We encourage you to engage in the following tasks to assure proper organization and coherence of ideas:

- Construct an outline that will identify the major sections and sub-sections of your report by headings and sub-headings.
- Identify the ideas associated with each heading.
- Group ideas that are connected and organize them in a logical order.
- Identify what analysis you will present as exhibits.
- Decide how to introduce and conclude your report.

The detailed structure of your report will depend on the nature of the case and on your analysis but will likely include an executive summary (see below), an introduction, the report body, and a conclusion plus exhibits. Exhibit 6-1 provides a checklist for the organization of a written case report.

Exhibit 6-1
CASE REPORT CHECKLIST

Title page
Table of contents
Executive summary
Issue statement
Data analysis
Alternatives analysis
Recommendations
Action and Implementation Plan
Exhibits

Write as a manager. As learning with cases aims to simulate real life, case reports tend to follow business conventions. In the business world, employees are expected to save time for their boss. Ease of reading is crucial, therefore, adopt a simple, functional style of writing. Clarity, brevity and accuracy must direct your writing. Make the information as transparent and quickly accessible as possible. Use short paragraphs, numerous headings and subheadings, point form lists; and clearly-labelled and well-referenced exhibits or appendixes to present data that support your points.

Business writing commonly calls for an executive summary as the frontispiece of the report, although it is normally written last. This summary should focus on your key recommendations. Assuming the president, or other senior executive, has only enough time to read this summary, what key points from your analysis and recommendations should this one page contain?

The rest of the report contains the analysis that leads to your recommendations. In the body of your report, which may include various types of quantitative and qualitative analyses, use case facts to support your arguments and conclusions. If you make assumptions, make sure that you identify them clearly and justify them fully (see Chapter 3 regarding assumptions).

In the alternative section of your report, discuss only legitimate alternatives, those directly linked to your analysis. It is common practice to start with the least acceptable alternative and build to the best. Consider the strengths, weaknesses as well as the consequences of each alternative. The length of treatment of each alternative should be a function of its worth. If an alternative has little merit, it deserves little space.

In the recommendation and action and implementation sections of your report, you must explain with consistency and logic why you recommend the alternative you chose and be as specific as possible in your plan of action.

Check your work. Proofread and review your work for accuracy in numbers and writing, including grammar, spelling and punctuation. Make sure your exhibits are properly labelled and referenced in the text.

Give it your best. Communicating in writing is an important part of most managers' work. Doing case reports will give you an excellent opportunity to practice expressing your ideas on paper. It is well worth giving it your best effort. The benefits of improving your written communication skills are enormous, as those skills are crucial in most fields, particularly in management.

CASE EXAMS

Types of Exam

Case exams may take various forms. They can be take-home or in-class exams, which can be either open or closed book exams. The case selected for the exam may be a recapitulation of a variety of previously discussed concepts, issues or aspects of the course; may focus only on one part of the material covered in the course; or may test how you can respond to a brand new situation.

If the students are asked to solve the case at home, the exam reverts to a case report, with perhaps a little more pressure, depending of the allotted period of time, from the moment the students receive it to the moment it has to be handed in. However, this kind of exam does not assure that the exam is in fact the student's own work. For this reason, the hybrid of take-home and in-class exam is sometimes used: a case is distributed for preparation ahead of time but the assignment questions are only given at the onset of the in-class exam.

If the main purpose of the exam is to test what students can do on their own or if they understand the main concepts of the course, then the case will likely be given in class with three to five hours to read and solve the case, as well as do the write-up. This type of exam is sometimes called a speed test, although notes and books are commonly allowed.

Whatever type of exam is given, your course review prior to receiving the exam case will be the same and should not entail too much work. Relax! Your on-going efforts throughout the course will now pay off. There is no need re-read all the cases of the course. It would be wise to review your Case Preparation Charts with reflection notes for each case however. Make sure you understand all the concepts and are comfortable with the various analytical tools that were used in the course. Ask for assistance if you do not understand something.

Specific suggestions on how to prepare for and write the two most common types of exam will be presented separately for each type. Suggestions that apply to all types of case exams follow.

Suggestions on How to Prepare for and Write an In-Class Exam

A) With the Case Handed out ahead of Time

Prepare the same way as you would for a case report. Follow the guidelines and suggestions offered in Chapter 3 on case preparation and be as thorough as possible.

Try to anticipate what types of questions will be asked and what analyses could be required. If throughout the course you have followed the suggested preparation format, starting with the Short Cycle Process, some of these questions will be obvious and will help you focus on the key issues as well as develop pertinent answers to them. Review the theory that may apply to the case and make sure that you are comfortable with the analytical tools that you may have to use.

Review your after class reflection notes of cases that may have similarities with this one. Of course, you do not need to re-read old cases and review their detailed analyses. You do not have enough time. But since you know what the case exam entails, you can target your review of previous case analyses that seem relevant by referring to your Case Preparation Charts.

Make detailed notes of your answers to all the anticipated questions as well as of your various analyses; and organize these notes carefully. You may conduct various quantitative and qualitative analyses. It is wise to be as comprehensive as possible but make sure each piece of analysis is properly labelled, easy to retrieve, and that your notes are well organized. You may also generate a comprehensive list of alternatives and evaluate each of them. You may prepare a detailed implementation plan for your preferred alternative. Even if you are not allowed to bring notes and materials in class, your prior work will be helpful.

Meet with your small group (if permitted). Following the small group discussion guidelines (see Chapter 4), a brief meeting or phone consultation with your small group may be particularly effective to check out your understanding of the case and build up your confidence. The small group discussion is not the place to start preparing and analyzing the case. Remember, you will be on your own for the exam.

If you have prepared well, your exam is strictly a question of organizing your ideas and conveying them effectively. Your instructor expects a product that demonstrates the quality of your preparation.

Tailor you answers. You may have to adjust your preparation notes to meet the specifics of the questions.

B) With the Case Handed out at the Start of the Exam

Manage your time wisely. Normally you will spend at least half of your time reading and analyzing the case. Use the Short Cycle Process and the other suggestions offered in Chapter 3 to be as effective as possible. Only when you have completed the analysis are you ready to write.

If you feel overwhelmed by the task at hand, you may wish to start your analysis by doing what will make you feel good, after having completed the Short Cycle Process. A good way to prevent panic is to follow a structured approach. That is why we suggest always starting with the six steps of the Short Cycle Process (see Chapter 3). Afterwards, if the feeling of uneasiness persists, you may want to play on your strengths. For some it may be a piece of qualitative analysis, such as consumer analysis; for others it may be some quantitative work, such as a break-even analysis. However, make sure your analysis relates to the main issue(s) of the case or the assigned questions.

Think about how to present your analysis before starting to write. We recommend that you spend several minutes on deciding how to present your written analysis. A good way to proceed is to make a list of your key findings and conclusions first and then to provide the evidence or arguments for each one. We encourage you to limit yourself to a few key points that will be well substantiated to demonstrate the depth of your analysis. In other words, it is better to focus on quality that quantity when you are ready to write, as tempting as it may be to fill as many pages as you can.

If you are allowed to bring notes and other materials to class, you may bring them for a sense of security, but be aware that they will likely be of little use to you. The learning should be integrated by now and you can lose a lot of time searching for an elusive thought, concept or model.

Suggestions That Apply to All Types of Case Exams

Find out and meet your instructor's expectations. Here is a list of such expectations:

a) a clear identification of the issue, decision, challenge, opportunity or problem facing the decision maker;
b) the ability to distinguish between problems and symptoms; causes and effects; and facts and opinions;
c) avoidance of case facts repetition without analysis or implications;

d) creativity in formulating alternatives;
e) rational analysis of each alternative in line with sound decision criteria;
f) well substantiated recommendations addressing the identified issue;
g) explicit and comprehensive action and implementation plan.

If marks allocated to each question are indicated, plan your time accordingly. This means that your first task is to prepare a timetable. Make sure you stick to it.

Make sure your analysis answers the questions. Read the questions carefully.

Don't worry too much about form. Elegance of style is not a prime consideration and writing in point form is normally acceptable. Focus your energy on the content and on writing your points clearly and simply. There may not be much time for editing.

Do not bring someone else's notes to class. By now you know that learning with cases is an individual process and cannot be borrowed. You will lose your precious time trying to make sense of someone else's thinking.

Resist the temptation of digressions. Although digressions may be good page fillers, focus your attention strictly on what is asked for. It is preferable to submit a short exam that addresses directly the issue(s) at stake than a long one that rambles a lot. For the marker, brevity is a virtue.

Support your recommendations quantitatively, if applicable. By substantiating your points with calculations, tables or charts, you may not only provide evidence that clarifies the issues, but also add variety and demonstrate your proficiency.

Hand-in all your exhibits and calculations. Some instructors suggest using the left-hand page of the exam booklet for calculations, additions or corrections. If your calculations do not work, they can always be crossed out and the marker will ignore them. You may wish to hand in your scratch paper and working notes if you feel they contain valuable information you did not have time to include in your exam paper.

Refer to theory or to real life practice, if it applies. Indicating your ability to apply knowledge and experience adds credibility to your work.

Be consistent. Make sure that the arguments used to accept or reject an alternative are consistent with the assumptions and calculations made, and are consistent with the prior interpretation of case information.

If using a personal computer, beware of too much inconsequential analysis. The temptation may be strong to perform calculations or mathematical analyses before you are sure they are necessary or useful.

Resist any temptation to share any type of information of any form during the in-class exam. The learning format proposed in this book involves a lot of sharing. In-class exams are the one exception to this philosophy of learning. Communication between students during any such exams constitutes cheating. It is not worth compromising your future by forgoing this fundamental rule.

Success with case exams is not a matter of good luck. It is the reward for regular class preparation throughout the course, extensive practice in all aspects of decision making, familiarity with analytical tools and the ability to translate your ideas into words. As you know, cases do not normally have right or wrong answers. The quality of your solution depends largely on your decision making skills. If you have developed them well through regular sound preparation, the long term benefits you will reap will accompany the good exam marks you will get.

A NOTE ABOUT GRADES FOR WRITTEN WORK

It is common knowledge that various small group members who have jointly worked on a case report or exam beforehand may receive substantially different individual exam grades. It is useful practice to compare your report or exam to that of your small group members to see why and where differences occur that may account for a substantial difference in grade. It is generally the richness of the explanations and the logic that explain the discrepancies. One person may write, "Ms. Jones faces a problem." Another may write, "I, as Ms. Jones, face a problem which, if left unresolved, could bankrupt this organization in less than a year." These statements are not equal.

Someone may write, "There are five alternatives which should be considered" and proceed to give a full page to each. Another may write, "There are five potential alternatives, three of which have little merit. They are: 1..., 2..., and 3... and this is why they should not be taken seriously... The remaining two are both sound and I will discuss each fully before making my recommendation."

Often students are afraid to take firm positions. They write about twenty problems and thirty solutions as if all merit equal attention. This lack of selectivity is a sure way to avoid getting a good grade.

It is the very ability to distinguish the important and the urgent, the short and the long term, the immediate from the basic, and the preferred from the less desirable that creates the power of persuasion and insight that produce superior grades.

managing your learning process

The case solving process has allowed me to develop skills for learning the rest of my life.

I have seen first hand where theory meets practice.

I do not mind admitting that I struggled through this process, but now I am seeing the benefits of my work.

These quotes from three recent graduates are ones we hope you can repeat when you complete your case course or program.

Professor Frank Folts at the Harvard Business School in discussing his expectations of the MBA students at time of graduation said, "As long as they can learn from their future experiences, we have accomplished what we wanted."

The effective manager learns continuously and allocates time and effort appropriately. Critical thinking skills, not the simple pursuit of management fads, make the difference between successful and less successful managers. Managers need to assess every situation individually, identify the problems, issues, challenges, opportunities or decisions involved and define appropriate decision criteria and alternatives. The basics of sound decision making and problem solving require continuous attention, practice and persistence. Case solving tasks can be seen as a process and managed as a process. It is a learnable and improvable process. Following the steps suggested in this text has both short and long-term pay-offs.

Learning is always the learning of "something." There is no such thing as learning itself. This concluding chapter summarizes the key ideas in learning with cases offered earlier.

CASES AND THE CASE METHOD

The case method is discussion-based learning where the cases provide the focus for deliberation and the joint stakeholders are instructors and students. Our reference to cases throughout this text has been to real, field-based "stories" faced by practitioners and released for educational purposes. Remember the cadaver analogy: cases are to management students (or whatever discipline you are studying) what real bodies are to medical students — an opportunity to practice harmlessly. Students in a protected case classroom get a chance to stretch, test, push, fend and grow so that when the door opens, they can enter the world prepared for the challenges ahead.

Cases and the case method require learning by doing and by teaching others. *Learning With Cases* provides two key frameworks to allow you to build a repertoire of possible analytical approaches and skills to communicate your views.

THE TWO KEY FRAMEWORKS

The two key frameworks presented in this text are: the Case Difficulty Cube and the Three Stage Learning Process.

The Case Difficulty Cube

The Case Difficulty Cube provides a way of classifying the educational challenges in the cases you read. The analytical dimension establishes the nature of your decision making task. The conceptual dimension relates to concepts, theories or techniques that you will have to know and apply. The presentation dimension relates to the provision and organization of information contained in the case.

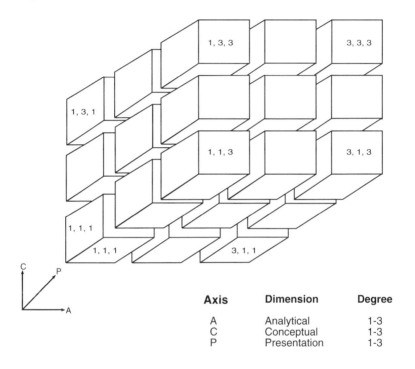

Axis	Dimension	Degree
A	Analytical	1-3
C	Conceptual	1-3
P	Presentation	1-3

Classifying cases on these three dimensions allows you to save time by preventing an aimless reading and wandering around in the data of the case. You will have a better sense of what you are doing. You can also focus your attention on where to concentrate to produce maximum benefit. The higher the degree of difficulty on any dimension, the more time you need to spend on the tasks related to that dimension.

The Three Stage Learning Process

The three stage learning process starts with your individual preparation. There is no substitute for this part: no hand-off to someone else, no just going to class and picking up the notes, no short-cuts around this personal responsibility for what you learn. Your commitment to regular, day-by-day individual preparation is fundamental to effective learning with cases.

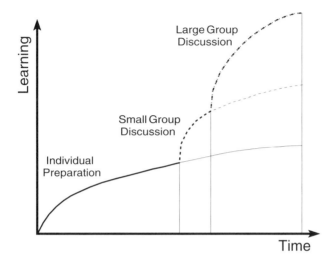

A second personal commitment is to attend and participate in a small group discussion of each case. This commitment is the first opportunity to test your performance on one of the fundamental reasons for using cases: learning by teaching. The members of your small group provide a ready audience for you to teach your understanding, your views and your use of tools and concepts. There is an equal opportunity to continue your learning by listening carefully to others as they teach you. Those students who commit to a planned, short, regular exchange of views on each case in a small group discussion will distinguish themselves from others in superior learning, better team management skills and increased self-confidence.

The third commitment you make in the three stage learning process is to attend and contribute to the large group discussion about each case. This part is the more public opportunity to learn by teaching, to add to the collective wisdom of the whole group, to test your preparation and delivery against a sample of the peer group you may professionally deal with in your future career. If you can do well in the case classroom you can do well in the real world. Doing well means to be active in contributing, listening, questioning and responding. It is unproductive and unfair just to be a sponge and silently drink in everyone else's wisdom. Your peers will want an equitable exchange. Following a regular routine around this three stage learning process will make you a welcome and equal partner, and a dependable, quality performer.

INDIVIDUAL PREPARATION

Most beginning students engage in learning with cases as follows: they just start reading a case, underline a few things, come to the end and say, "Hum, that's interesting, now what am I supposed to do?" So they read it again, underline a few more things, come to the end and say, "Wow, this stuff is pretty neat, what am I supposed to do now?" By the third or fourth reading, everything is underlined, everything is critical, three hours have gone by and they are not much further ahead. Besides, there are two more cases to read plus a chapter in the book and two articles for tomorrow. The beginning students come quickly to the conclusion that they do not learn anything with cases. Frustration and anxiety get established early and it is hard to stop the negative spiral.

When preparing a case do not just read and re-read cases aimlessly. Do not try to memorize the facts of the case. There is a better way. We have introduced the Short and Long Cycle Processes and the Case Preparation Chart to assist your individual preparation. As you gain experience in case preparation, you will develop your own variations and guides. At the outset, if you do not know where you are going, our road map can help you.

Individual preparation starts with the Short Cycle Process (see Chapter 3 and Exhibit 3-1). The maximum time required is 15 minutes for this process. Its purpose is to find out: Whose position are you in? What is your current challenge or concern? Why are you dealing with it now? When do you have to decide? Where does this case fit on the Case Difficulty Cube? After the Short Cycle Process is completed, let the thoughts and ideas "soak in" as you reflect on the nature of the case: Are the initial answers to these questions clear or not so clear? Is this issue(s) familiar or not? What is your initial comfort zone with the challenge(s) presented? The Short Cycle Process gets you focussed to address the situation you have been parachuted into.

Individual preparation next moves into the Long Cycle Process (see Chapter 3 and Exhibit 3-1). This Long Cycle Process starts with a careful reading of the case. This reading is not for the purpose of memorizing the story. The objective is to focus on the key issue(s) and the information relevant to the seven steps in the case solving process. Remember that the case analysis process will consume you if you let it. You can always spend more time analyzing, albeit with diminishing returns. Set appropriate time limits and stick to them. For every hour you spend in class discussing a case, spend one to two focused hours in individual preparation. When the time is up, tell yourself you are finished, "I have given this case quality attention but now I am done and must move on to other things." Routinely completing the Long Cycle Process will put you on a learning curve to improved performance with every case you tackle.

Be sure to use the Case Preparation Chart (see Exhibit 3-2 in Chapter 3). This chart is your road map to locate where you are, to emphasize the important conclusions, to convey the key parts of your decision analysis, and to form the basis for your notes from which you will teach your views and understandings to others in the subsequent small and large group discussions.

SMALL GROUP DISCUSSION

The small group discussion is the vital link between individual preparation and large group discussion. Small group discussion is hard work. When you are teaching someone who simultaneously wants to teach you, effective communication and listening are paramount. The quality of the small group discussion depends on your ability to bring out the best assets that your small group can produce and to dissipate its worst liabilities. Remember to take some time and expend some care in forming your group: look for a range of resources, experiences and diversity. Recognize that small group discussions may produce conflicts and "jockeying for position." Revisit periodically your group process. Achieve agreement on the small group guidelines. Renew commitments in small group discussion. Harness the added learning power in a small group and help your group to maximize performance.

Avoid two bad habits! The first bad habit is skipping the small group discussion part of the learning process except for major presentations, assignments and formal reports. Regular short meetings will produce big dividends. The second bad habit is assigning one case to each person for a major work-up while the rest of the members just skim the cases assigned for a given day or week. Your learning with cases will be maximized when you do by yourself the necessary work on all the cases assigned.

And one last reminder. Allow "soak time" after the small group discussion to reflect on all the views expressed and the analyses offered to up-date your Case Preparation Chart. You will know where you have support in your small group and you will be able to acknowledge the contributions of your small group colleagues to your learning in the large group discussion.

LARGE GROUP DISCUSSION

The classroom is the third major stage in the process of learning with cases. The large group discussion gives you a chance to contribute what you have learned in your individual preparation and small group discussion. The classroom presents the opportunity for you to put your views and evidence out to be questioned and juried by your peers. However, you may be one of the students who is terrified, reluctant, naturally quiet or who simply wants to avoid talking in large groups. Case discussion classes can be intimidating and unnatural compared to typical business meetings. You can, nevertheless, help yourself reduce this fear and take advantage of the opportunities to maximize your contributions to the large group discussion.

As stated in Chapter 5, the following ideas may be helpful for participating in large group discussions.

- Nothing, but nothing, beats individual preparation and small group discussion in building your understanding and confidence regarding your evidence and justification for positions taken on case analyses. This state of readiness is the definition of good luck. Good luck occurs when preparation meets opportunity.

- Use your Case Preparation Chart as a road map for where the class discussion is, where it has been and where it seems to be going. Tick-off the points already raised. Re-emphasize those points only casually offered by others or in fact missed entirely.

- Do not be afraid to direct and steer the class discussion by moving forward or backward in the decision making process. Contributions around directing class discussion can be just as valuable as contributions around case content.

- Be an active listener and use your thinking speed to review what speakers have offered so far and preview what still needs to be said.

- Choose your position in the class carefully. Do not automatically gravitate toward the back. Sitting near the front will help to reduce the physical size of the class. Having direct eye contact and talking directly to one or two of your favorite colleagues will help to reduce the size of the class psychologically.

- Allow for reflection time after class to update your Case Preparation Chart. Reflect on your preparation versus the class position at the end of the class. Where did you agree and disagree and why? What did you do well or poorly in your individual preparation and in your small group and why? If you cannot determine the answers to these questions, get some help and advice either from your classmates or from your instructor.

VARIATIONS

The central theme in this book is that learning with cases can be effectively accomplished through individual preparation, small group discussion and large group discussion, a repeatable standard process. The common variations around the standard process are making formal case presentations in class, preparing formal case reports to be handed in and writing case exams (see Chapter 6). Even with these variations and regardless of instructors' objectives, individual case preparation is a fundamental first prerequisite that will provide the solid foundation upon which to build any of the particular variations desired.

You will face, nonetheless, some particular challenges in courses where only a few cases are assigned. Here, instructors are using cases more for variety and illustration. The problem you will have in these instances is the lack of opportunity to practice using the tools of your trade. The three stage learning process and the associated steps still are useful and will steer you in the right direction. There just are not as many iterations to help you move along the learning curve.

CONCLUSION

This book is about the process of learning with cases. It does not concern itself with the specific content of the course(s) you may be following. Of course, there is a connection. The better control you have over the process of learning with cases, the easier it will be to absorb the course specific theoretical and conceptual content. It is not a trade-off: "Should I spend time doing the case or learn the theory?" It is a win-win proposition instead. You can do both well and still be assured you are getting the best learning results possible in the minimum time required.

Actions speak louder than words. This phrase applies to you. Your actions will confirm your commitment to the repetitive routine of individual preparation, small group discussion and large group discussion. Practicing your skills and abilities in decision-making in the case discussion classroom will ultimately differentiate your performance as a professional.

Learning with cases is hard work that leads to personal achievement and satisfaction. There is no rule against hard work being fun. We have tried to arouse your imagination in helping you to explore unfamiliar situations, to experience the stress in decision-making under uncertainty, and to practice the art and science of management (or other profession). We have tried to reduce your frustration and anxiety by making learning with cases easier, more meaningful, more operationally specific, more valuable, and more pleasurable.

references

Barnes, Louis B., Christensen, C. Roland, Hansen, Abby J., *Teaching and the Case Method: Text, Cases, and Readings*, 3rd ed., Harvard Business School, Boston, Mass., 1994.

Christensen, C. Roland, Garvin, David A., and Sweet, Ann, *Education for Judgment, The Artistry of Discussion Leadership*, Harvard Business School Press, Boston, Mass., 1991.

Christensen, C. Roland, Hansen, Abby J., *Teaching and the Case Method*, Harvard Business School Press, Boston, Mass., 1987.

Conner, Marcia L., Clawson, James G., editors, *Creating a Learning Culture: Strategy, Technology, and Practice*, Cambridge University Press, 2004.

Easton, Geoff, *Learning from Case Studies*, Second Edition, Prentice Hall International(UK) Ltd, London, England, 1992.

Erskine, James A., Leenders, Michiel R., Mauffette-Leenders, Louise A., *Teaching with Cases*, 3rd ed., Richard Ivey School of Business, London, Canada, 2003.

Gilmore, T. N., Schall, E., "Staying Alive to Learning: Integrating Enactments with Case Teaching to Develop Leaders," *Journal of Policy Analysis and Management*, 1996, 15, 3, 444-56.

IMD, *Mastering Executive Education*, FT Prentice Hall, Great Britain, 2005.

Lantis, Jeffrey S., Kuzma, Lynn M., Boehrer, John, editors, *The New International Studies Classroom: Active Teaching, Active Learning*, Lynn Rienner, Boulder, 2000.

Leenders, Michiel R., Mauffette-Leenders, Louise, Erskine, James A., *Writing Cases*, 4th ed., Richard Ivey School of Business, London, Canada, 2001.

Lynn, Lawrence E., *Teaching and Learning with Cases: A Guidebook*, Chatham House Publishers Inc., U.S., 1999

Lundeberg, Mary A., Levin, Barbara B., Harrington, Helen L., *Who Learns What from Cases and How? The Research Base for Teaching and Learning with Cases*, Lawrence Erlbaum Assoc. Inc, Mahwah, 1999.

Maister, David A., "How to Avoid Getting Lost in the Numbers," 682-010, Harvard Business School, Boston, Mass., 1981.

Shapiro, Benson P., "Hints for Case Teaching," HBS Case Services, Harvard Business School, Boston, Mass., 1984.

Vance, Charles M., *Mastering Management Education, Innovations in Teaching Effectiveness*, Sage Publications, Newbury Park, California, 1993.

index

Action and Implementation Plan,
    36, 53-54, 81-82, 115
  basic questions, 53, 81-82
  lack of time, 53
  milestones, 36, 54
  misplaced concreteness, 54
Advisor, students; *see*
    Counselling
Alternative, 36, 38-39, 46-53, 81,
    114
  Analysis Matrix, 49
  analysis of, 49-52
  assessment, 36, 49-52, 115
  decision tree, 50-51
  evaluation; *see* assessment
  generating, 36, 46-47, 114
  predicting outcomes, 50-51
  preferred, 36, 38, 52-53
  pros and cons, 49, 53, 114
  selection, 52-53, 54
  short vs long term,
    considerations, 50
Analysis, case, 34, 40-54
  causes and effects, 36, 40, 43-45
  constraints and opportunities,
    40, 45, 47
  quantitative and qualitative
    assessment, 45-46, 51-52, 115
  steps, 40
  techniques and tools, 40, 80
Armchair cases, 2-3
Assignment, case, 30-32
  other types, 31
  questions, 32, 34, 35
  specific, 32
  standard, 30
Assumptions, 36, 54-56, 89, 110
  hidden, 55
  kinds, 55-56
  making, 55

Case, 1-9, 29, 120
  analysis, 34, 40-54
  assignments, 30-32, 39

competition, 104
context, 3, 38
data, 2; *see also* Information
date, 3
definition, 2
discussion; *see* Large
    group discussion
exhibits, 35
formats, 2, 16
location, 3
normal outline, 37-40
opening paragraph, 33-34, 37-38
organization, 37-40
reader's role, 31; *see also*
    Decision maker's role
reading, 20, 32, 35, 37-40, 58, 123
release, 2, 120
series, 57
size-up, 34
solving process; *see* analysis
urgency, 42
variants, 103-117, 127-128
writer, 8, 37
Case Difficulty Cube, 11-18, 36,
    120-121
  analytical dimension, 12-14, 57,
    120
  conceptual dimension, 14-15,
    121
  degrees of difficulty, 16-18, 121
  presentation dimension, 15-16,
    121
Case Method, 1-9, 120
  expectations, 7-8
Case Preparation Chart, 35, 36, 43,
    44, 52, 58, 59-60, 66, 73, 92, 98,
    99, 112, 123-124, 126
Christensen, C. Roland, 76, 84, 88,
    90, 94, 101
Class discussion; *see* Large
    group discussion
Communication skills, 6, 22, 27,
    111

Computer graphics, 2, 45, 105-106
Confidentiality; *see* Ethics
Contingency theory, 38
Contribution; *see* Participation
Counselling, 71-72, 96

Data, 2; *see also* Information
    analysis, 43-46, 80
Decision, 8, 39, 81
    criteria, 47-48, 49, 54, 56
    definition, 6
Decision maker's role, 20, 21, 31
Decision Tree Diagram, 50-51
Discrimination, 99
Discussion, case; *see also*
        Large group discussion
    phases, 76-83
    process variations, 76
    roles, 92-93
    start, 78-79, 95
Diversity, 71, 98-99, 125
    cultural differences, 71, 98
    value differences, 71, 99

Easton, Geoff, 73, 86, 92, 105
Ethics, 7, 83-84, 100-101, 115-116
    case disguise, 84
    civility, 90
    class notes, 101, 115
    confidentiality, 2, 7, 84, 101, 116
Evaluation; *see also* Reflection
    grades, 27, 53, 85, 116, 117
    of case content, 100
    of group, 100
    of participation, 85
    of self, 100, 127
    of written work, 117
Exams, case, 6, 99, 111-116, 127
    cheating, 116
    course review, 111-112
    suggestions, 112-116
    types, 111-112
Exercises; *see* Armchair cases
Exhibits, case, 35, 40

Financial statements, 35, 40

Folts, Frank, 119
Frederick, Peter, 101

Grades; *see* Evaluation

Hansen, Abby J., 94, 101
Harvard Business School, 46, 76,
    85, 119

Implementation Plan; *see* Action
    and Implementation
Importance and Urgency Matrix,
    36, 43
Individual preparation, 20-21, 22,
    29-60, 121-124, 126
    importance of, 20, 29, 121-122,
        126-127
    long cycle process, 34, 35-54, 58,
        68, 123-124
    short cycle process, 32-35, 36,
        41, 58-59, 112-114
    tips, 57-59
Information, case, 4, 35-39
    background, 37-39
    data analysis, 43-46, 80
    facts vs opinions, 37, 44, 86, 114
    incompleteness, 4
    missing, 15-16, 36, 54-55
    organization, 16, 35, 37-40
    sorting, 15
    specific area of interest, 39
    qualitative vs quantitative, 44,
        80
Instructor, 8, 78, 83-85, 91, 96
    definition, 8
    directive, 78, 84, 91
    evaluation, 85
    expectations, 91
    non-directive, 78, 84
    role, 84
    solution, 83-84, 89
Issue, case, 36, 41-43, 79-80, 114
    basic, 36, 41-42
    definition, 41-43
    identification, 79-80, 114
    immediate, 36, 41-42

importance, 42-43
Importance and Urgency
    Matrix, 36, 43
urgency, 42-43

Language difficulties, 98
Large group discussion, 9, 24-27,
    75-101, 122-123, 126-127
    contributing when not certain,
        96-97
    process, 76
        case discussion, 78-82
        in-class-pre-class, 76-77
        post-case, 82-84
        pre-case, 77
    purposes, 25, 126
    sitting position, 95, 127
    stakeholders, 84-85, 120
    useful contributions, 79-83
Learned, E. P., 94
Learning
    by doing, 3, 26, 99, 120
    by teaching, 3, 7, 21, 26, 68, 84,
        120, 122, 123
    quality,19-20, 24, 25
    quantity, 19-20, 24, 25
Learning process, 1, 11, 18-28, 121
    123, 127
    individual preparation, 20-22,
        29-60, 121-124, 126
    large group discussion, 9, 24-27,
        75-101, 122-123, 126-127
    small group discussion, 21-24,
        61-74, 103, 122, 125, 126
Listening, effective, 6, 22, 91, 93-94
Long Cycle Process, 34, 35-54, 58,
    68, 123-124
    analyzing the case, 40-56
    reading of the case, 37-40, 124

Maister, David A., 46, 59
Management School of the
    University of Lancaster, 86
Missing information, 15-16, 36,
    54-55

Note-taking, 6, 37, 59, 66, 94

Organization chart; *see* Exhibits

Participant, 8, 85
    responsibilities, 85, 101
Participation
    challenges, dealing with, 95-99,
        126
    content contributions, 86, 126
    contribution agenda, 68, 73
    discussion roles, 92-93
    effectiveness, 86-89
    evaluation, 27
    fear, 23, 25, 95-96, 126-127
    ineffectiveness, 89-90
    inputs to class, 92-93
    listening, effective, 86, 91, 93-94
    note-taking, 94-95
    process contributions, 86-87, 126
    quality vs quantity, 88
    raising your hand, 87, 96
    reasons for, 26-27
    strategies and tactics, 91-99
    timing, 92
    wrong answers, 26, 88, 116
Preparation, case; *see also*
        Individual preparation
    lack of, 98
    notes, 92, 107, 124; *see also* Case
        Preparation Chart
    time, 18, 29, 124
Presentations, case, 103-107, 127
    critic-observers, 106-107
    non-presenters' roles, 104
    suggestions for, 105-106
    types of, 103-104
    visual aids, 106, 107
Problem; *see* Issue
Problem solving model; *see also*
        Analysis, case
    evaluation of results, 56-57
Professional conduct, code of, 7;
    see also Ethics

Quantitative
    analysis, 45-46, 115
    suggestions for calculations, 46
    vs qualitative assessment, 49-52

Reading of the case, 20, 32, 35,
        37-40, 58, 123
Readings, additional, 20, 59, 77,
        123
Reflection
    after class, 27-28, 57, 99-100, 127
    after Short Cycle Process, 35,
        125
    after small group, 57, 65, 72-73
    notes, 73, 112
Reports, case, 6, 107-111, 127
    assignment, 108
    check list, 109
    evaluation criteria, 108
    executive summary, 109-110
    organization, 109
    suggestions, 108-111
    types, 107-108
    writing style, 109-110
Role playing, 98, 104

Shapiro, Benson P., 85
Short Cycle Process, 32-35, 36, 41,
        58-59, 112-114, 123-124
    purposes, 33-34, 124
    steps, 33-35
Size-up, case, 34
Skills, inventory of, 5-6, 86, 120
    analytical, 5, 38
    application, 5
    creative, 6
    decision making, 5, 116, 119, 128
    interpersonal, 6, 122
    oral, 6, 22; *see also*
        communication
    social, 6, 122
    time management, 6
    written communication, 6, 111
Small group, 9, 21-24, 61-74, 103,
        122, 125
    bad habits, 23, 125
    composition, 63
    consensus, 67, 103
    dealing with problems, 70-72
    discussion, 67-68
    guidelines, 65-67, 71
    leader, 66

location, 65
organizing for, 62-65
problems, identification, 68-70
reasons for, 21-23, 62, 122
reflection after, 57, 65, 72-73
rotation, 63
secretary, 66
size, 62
spokesperson, 66-67, 103
teleconferencing, 65, 113
time, 23, 24, 64, 67
timing, 65
Starting class, 78-79, 95
    effective ways, 79
Student, 8, 101; *see also*
        Participant

Teacher; *see* Instructor
Teamwork; *see* Small group
Time, 11, 21, 37, 83, 124; *see also*
        Preparation,
    constraints, 11
    management, 58, 64, 68-69, 83,
        108, 113
Teaching objectives, 3
Theory, 4, 14, 20, 77, 80, 112, 116,
        121

Vance, Charles M., 68
Visual aids, 106, 107

Wild, Bud, 25